Whisper

FINDING **GOD IN** THE **EVERYDAY**

DANIELLE BEAN

ASCENSION

West Chester, Pennsylvania

Ascension
PO Box 1990
West Chester, PA 19380
1-800-376-0520
ascensionpress.com

Cover design by Rosemary Strohm

Printed in the United States of America
21 22 23 24 25 5 4 3 2 1
ISBN 978-1-950784-65-3

CONTENTS

Where God Waits

I used to wake up while it was still dark, change into sweats in a cold bathroom, open up my laptop, and hit PLAY. Then I punched and kicked, jumped and lifted for the better part of an hour.

I used to take sixty-eight calls a day, chasing deadlines and running on adrenaline. I talked fast, overpromised, and rolled my eyes at questions from people who, for whatever reason, didn't keep up.

I used to strap one baby to my body while holding another in my arms while another tugged on my sleeve and two more fought over whose turn it was to choose the next storybook.

I used to fly through grocery aisles, filling my cart with basics and hurrying to swipe my card so that I could get home and throw some of that stuff into a pot before dinnertime.

I used to rush to church, kneel in a pew, and then sit back in wonder as my mind zipped from here to there and then back again, never pausing for a breath. Because I never did either.

And maybe that's why it feels so good to do what I do now. Which is to pause sometimes, and breathe.

I still do lots of things, maybe even too many things, but I do less. I do less with more intention and deliberation, more care and attention. I do less, but look more people in the eyes. I do less, but think more things through. I type out thoughtful answers to emails I would have deleted years ago because there simply wasn't time. I don't roll my eyes so much, and my jaw almost never aches at the end of the day because I've been unthinkingly clenching it for several hours.

I know God was with me back when I was going so fast and striving so hard, but I can't help but think he was waiting for me, too. Waiting for me to slow down and settle in. Waiting for me to look him in the eyes. Waiting for me to stop striving and start diving more deeply. Waiting for the me I am now.

And now that I can see how some of this works, now that I can see a little bit of where this is going, I squint into the future sometimes. I want to see the me that I will be then. When I catch a glimpse of her, I smile. Because I know God, ever patient and outside of time, is waiting for her, too.

I want to go there. I want to go to that place where God is waiting.

The other day, I was talking with a friend, another writer and mom who, like me, has been married for over twenty-five years. She shared that in a recent conversation with her mother, she observed that there are many younger writers these days, and that perhaps it was time for her to write less, in order to make room for new voices.

"Don't do that!" Her mother had interrupted her thoughts. "You finally have something to say!"

And I think maybe that is what is prompting me to write this particular book. After all these years, after all these words, I might finally have something to say.

One thing I want to say is that God is with us. Now that my life is quieter and slower, I see God and experience God in new ways. After all these years of striving and chasing after God, I feel like I am only just now realizing that the place where God is waiting is right here. And he's been here all along.

A priest who is a friend of mine once wrote a review of one of my books in which he called me an "everyday mystic," someone who sees God in the everyday stuff of life. Those words stood out to me because I do want to be that. I want to be an "everyday mystic," not because I want a fancy label, but because that's what I think God wants for me. That's what God wants for every one of us.

But I need to work on it. I need to work on sitting still and looking around me. When I do that, I can know that God is right here, so large and so close that I can't possibly take him all in. In those moments when I see that, I write notes in a journal or talk to my husband in the middle of the night or madly text a friend, all the while thinking, "I need to tell someone about this!"

So maybe that's what this book is. Me telling you about this.

I used to think that the ultimate goal in life was to seek God, and that it was a hard task. I needed to look through murky waters and strain my eyes to find God. I needed to shout toward the heavens in order to make my voice heard. God was on the other side of a great chasm, and I needed to figure out how to make my way across it.

I sometimes read about the lives of great saints and mystics and feel a little bit envious. I mean, when Jesus appears to you in the bedroom of your convent, there is no confusion. There is no wondering about where God is and what his will for you might be. He's right there, standing at the foot of your bed, talking to you and telling you what to do. When you experience rhapsodies during meditation, when you can levitate and bilocate, when you miraculously heal people and read their souls, there is no room for doubt or distraction. You know God is with you, and you are on the right path.

But what about the rest of us? The rest are left struggling here, seeking God and wondering what he wills for us. We are left striving.

It's the striving that I have come to see as unnecessary. What if the ultimate goal in life is not so much to find God, but to find out that he is right here? What if we don't need to seek God so much as we need to stop, open our eyes, open our hearts, and allow ourselves to be found? What if God is looking for us, and yet in all our striving and seeking, we keep running away?

God isn't appearing at the foot of my bed in shining white robes. His voice isn't booming from the clouds above. But he is here. He is with us. There is so much God wants to say to us, so much he wants to show us, so many ways he wants to be present to us, comfort us, challenge us, and love us. All we everyday mystics need to do is open our eyes to see it.

Will you stop striving and seeking? Will you sit down with me instead? Let's be still together. Let's stop doing and start being. Let's be everyday mystics, and allow ourselves to be found.

CHAPTER ONE

Breaking Boundaries: Encountering God in Other People

There was something different about Kelly.

The night I met her at a women's social gathering, she and I connected at the snack table, where I was helping the hostess slice banana bread and set it out on plates.

"I've seen you before," she said, and then launched into a detailed story about how her cat was sick and she wasn't sure she would be able to get to the vet to pick up the medicine because she didn't like to drive anymore.

I could not remember having seen this woman before. She probably wasn't much older than me, but her hair was unbrushed, and her mismatched pieces of clothing hung on her body like they were bought for someone else. She was undeniably out of place at this gathering, where most of the other women wore leggings with cute boots and pretty scarves.

Her brown eyes locked onto mine with unnerving intensity as she told me about the job she used to have. It was a good job, she told me, because she could walk to it, even though she had a car, one that her estranged mother had given her years ago.

As she poured another cup of coffee, I looked over her shoulder and caught sight of my friend, Meghan, who smiled and waved at me. I had not seen Meghan for weeks, and we had been texting that afternoon about how much we were looking forward to connecting that evening, to catch up with each other and share about what was going on in our lives and with our families. Between work and kids, it was hard for us to find time to talk, and monthly women's group meetings were a precious little bit of time we could share.

Over the course of the next thirty minutes, I tried a few times to make an excuse to leave the table and go find Meghan, but Kelly always had one more thing she needed to tell me. And so I learned about her troubled relationships, police encounters, and hospital stays.

When the meeting ended and most of the other women were gathering their things, putting on coats, and preparing to drive home, I told her that I really needed to go.

"I should get your number!" she said, her eyes darting around, in a sudden panic for something to write on. She raced to the coat rack, retrieved a giant tote bag overflowing with books and clothing, and pulled a crumpled piece of paper from it. She smoothed the paper on the table and then looked up at me expectantly, pen poised and ready to write.

"I really like talking with you," she said.

Those words stayed with me as I buttoned my coat and waved an "I'm sorry" goodbye to Meghan from across the parking lot.

Of course she likes talking to me! I thought, rolling my eyes. *I was a receptacle for her conversation.*

I got into the car, glanced at my phone, and saw a text from Meghan: "You are too nice!"

I wondered about that as I drove home. Was I too nice? Of all the women present there that night, why was I the one that

Kelly trapped by the banana bread? Why were my plans to see my friend interrupted by this stranger? Why did I give her my number? What would I do when she called?

I thought of Kelly. What kind of person tells a random stranger such personal things? What kind of person ignores all social cues and talks at someone like that for thirty minutes straight?

Even as I wondered, though, I knew the answer: A hurting person. A lonely person. A person without other options, that's what kind.

It is sometimes difficult for me to see God in other people, and yet he himself tells us that's precisely where he is.

"Then the righteous will answer him, 'Lord, when did we see you hungry and feed you, or thirsty and give you drink? And when did we see you a stranger and welcome you, or naked and clothe you? And when did we see you sick or in prison and visit you?' And the King will answer them, 'Truly, I say to you, as you did it to one of the least of these my brethren, you did it to me'" (Matthew 25:37-40).

Jesus' words could not be more clear. He knows about the human inclination to categorize people into groups of "worthy" and "unworthy." He knows about the "least of these," and tells us that it is God himself we meet in them.

I sometimes like to reflect on Jesus' words and apply them in more comfortable ways, to my everyday life, to my friends and family. And truthfully? That is often challenging enough.

Do I hear Jesus in a crying infant who keeps me awake at night? Do I see Jesus in a surly teenager or annoying coworker or irritable husband? I can think I am making great strides in seeing Jesus in others, but then someone like Kelly comes along to remind me of just how far I still have to go.

If I ran into Jesus at a social meeting, I probably would not begrudge him my time. I would be honored if he chose to chat with me over banana bread. Why would I be grateful to talk with Jesus, but not with Kelly? Why would I consider Meghan worthy of my time, but not Kelly? Why would I have not minded chatting with a new person at women's group if she had a stylish haircut and talked about "normal" things, like work deadlines and Little League?

Why do I categorize people into groups of "us" and "them"? Why, despite prayer time and Bible study, is it still sometimes so hard to see God where he is, where he tells us he waits for us ... in other people?

I first realized that I had a problem seeing people the way God does back when I was in college. I was the only freshman who passed the competitive application process to take part in a "spring break alternative" trip to an Appalachian county in Kentucky. I remember that the priest who was in charge of the trip took me aside at our first meeting to tell me that he found the essay I wrote in my application "deeply moving," that he would be awarding me a scholarship for my trip, and that he was grateful to have me joining the group.

I don't remember what I wrote in that essay, but I do remember driving over eighteen hours in a van with a dozen other college kids, sleeping on the floor of a gym, and then finally arriving at a small shack at the end of a dirt road where a woman named Wanda greeted us. She spoke with such a heavy drawl that I felt like I was in French class, trying to keep up with a foreign language. Wanda let us know that we would not have access to running water for the week, our shelter would be rough, and our food would be limited, so that we might experience a little bit of the kind of poverty suffered every day by the people we were there to serve.

It was a long week, but I felt pretty good about what we were doing. We spent our days cleaning up public areas, stacking wood and doing odd jobs for elderly people, cleaning out classrooms in a local school, and preparing and delivering food to families in need.

One day, some of us were assigned the task of picking up trash alongside a main road in the small town where we were staying. As we filled bag after bag with empty beer cans, fast-food wrappers, and rusty pieces of metal, I was astonished at how much garbage there was. We worked for hours under the blistering sun and had a long row of stuffed trash bags but only a tiny span of cleaned-up roadside to show for our efforts.

At one point in the day, a beat-up pickup truck rattled and slowed as it approached us. A large teenager leaned out of the driver's side window and snarled as he looked us over.

"That's right!" he shouted as he tossed an empty soda bottle in our direction. "Pick up my trash!"

He sped away laughing, and we stood, speechless, holding our bags of garbage.

Later that evening, when we met as a group to talk about our day, I kept quiet, but another student told Wanda about that moment and asked, "If these people don't even like us and can't even be polite, what are we doing here? Why are we trying to help?"

I thought Wanda would be aghast, or at least a little bit embarrassed by what had happened, but she did not appear to be.

"Did you come here to be liked?" she asked.

On the last afternoon of our stay, Wanda had some of us bring food and cleaning supplies to a local family. We arrived at a small house with a dilapidated front porch covered in stacks of newspapers and empty cat food cans. When we entered the kitchen, an older couple greeted us and introduced us to their son, Billy-Wayne. Billy-Wayne might have been about thirty years old.

He wore a greasy ball cap, overalls, and a wide smile that revealed missing teeth.

The group of us talked for a while, about family and church and the local news. We put some groceries in their small refrigerator and pantry, and then were preparing to leave when Billy-Wayne stopped us.

"I like this one," he said to his parents, as he gestured at me. "This one's pretty. This one seems like our kind of people."

Our kind of people.

I wasn't sure I wanted to be that, but I understood the deeper meaning of those words. I had gone into that week with the grandiose idea that I was going to do something helpful and important for the people who lived in impoverished Appalachia. I did not fully realize it as I stood in Billy-Wayne's kitchen, but the only important thing that was being accomplished that week was happening in my own heart.

God was helping me to understand that I tended to see human beings in categories, categories that he does not recognize. Just as Jesus tried to open others' hearts and minds when he sat down to eat with prostitutes and tax collectors, he was inviting me to see that Wanda, Billy-Wayne, and that angry teenager, as uncomfortable as they made me, were God in disguise. They were God asking, "Do you see me now? Can you love me here?"

If they could see me as their kind of people, could I see them as mine?

Of course, God's challenges to us are not always so dramatic and clear. For most of us, life is not an extended spring break alternative trip. I did return home. I graduated and got married and started a family, and yet even now, decades later, I recall God's challenge to see others as he does. God is not only in the people of Appalachia. He's in the everyday people he places in my everyday life, though I sometimes need to squint a bit to see him there.

I once woke up my husband in the middle of the night to announce that we were meant to be missionaries in Calcutta. My husband knows me well, and so he only sighed and said, "No, we are not. Go back to sleep."

The next morning I laughed at my middle-of-the-night epiphany and recognized that my work situation was stressful and we were going through a challenging phase with one of our teenagers. I was trying to escape to Calcutta of all places.

From our comfortable perspective, meeting God by working to serve the very obviously poor and needy can feel more glamorous sometimes than seeking him in the mundane needs of the people he places in our lives right now. I am unlikely to receive a humanitarian award for asking my husband if he would like me to make him lunch or for listening patiently to my teenage daughter's rant about the ways the world has wronged her, and yet these are the people I meet today. This is where God is waiting for me right now.

When my babies were small, I always cherished that time, as exhausting as it was, when they would spend endless hours in my arms or on my hip as we went about our days together. So closely were we connected, I remember thinking that I could not always tell where one of us ended and the other began. I knew what they wanted and what they needed often before they even asked for it.

I love reflecting on that bond, as a lesser experience of the kind of connection each of us is meant to have with God. I recall thinking about the immensity of the role I played in my small children's lives at that point and being daunted by it. I was like God to them, the one on whom they depended for their very existence, and the source of every good thing. It's a large task to be another human being's first experience of God.

As hard as it was to meet their every need, there was something natural and intensely satisfying about it as well. I was made to be their mom, and the instinctual drive to give to them, even at great cost to myself sometimes, was built in.

Other people are not my precious babies, and yet Jesus challenges me to see them that way sometimes. Can we meet God in the needs of other people? God does not separate people into categories when he reminds us of our worth.

"Are not two sparrows sold for a penny? And not one of them will fall to the ground without your Father's will. But even the hairs of your head are all numbered. Fear not, therefore; you are of more value than many sparrows" (Matthew 10:29-31).

God has the hairs on my head counted, but also on Kelly's. On Billy-Wayne's. On the heads of angry, hurting people who might lash out at us, even when we try to help. We are, each of us, worth more than many sparrows, and none of us falls to the ground without his notice. We are, all of us, God's kind of people.

I tried to remember this one recent day when I opened an email and saw an angry tirade filled with threats and foul language. It was jarring.

The sender, whom I did not know very well, was inexplicably furious over a small bill that hadn't been paid. I quickly paid the bill, deleted the email, and tried to forget about it, but the hurtful names and threats stuck with me. I could not stop thinking about it.

"What kind of person does that?" I wondered to myself and in conversation with friends. What kind of person gets so angry, is so unreasonable, and loses all control like that?

What kind of person? God's kind of person.

I imagine myself at the end of my life meeting God and asking, "Lord, when did I see you a stranger and not welcome you?"

"Don't you remember?" he might say. "I sent you that nasty email."

Or he might tell me that we met over coffee and banana bread at women's group. He might remind me of any number of times I have not considered others "my kind of people," or when I have attempted to draw lines between myself and others, considering only some worthy of my love and acceptance.

I have far to go. Many times, I want to see God in others and love God in others only when it feels good and looks as I think it should. When it's fair. When it's reasonable. When I'm comfortable.

Jesus does not come to make us comfortable. He comes to challenge us, and he is not far away. He is right beside us, living and breathing and asking for our love and attention right here, right now, in the everyday moments of everyday life. He's asking what's for dinner, and he needs a ride to baseball practice. He wants us to listen while he complains about that thing at work. He might be dressed funny and smell weird. Or maybe he's whiny and annoying, rude, hurtful, or demanding.

Each person is an invitation from God himself: Will you meet me here, inside of this precious person whose hairs are counted? Will you see me here in the "least of these"? Will you love me?

I want to say yes, Lord. I want to see you. I want to love you.
I want to embrace every kind of person as my kind of person
because they are yours. Give me eyes to see your face and
ears to hear your voice in the everyday people I meet, know,
and am called to love each day. Amen.

CHAPTER TWO

Tasting Goodness: Finding God in Joy

I'll never forget the first time my oldest son tasted a strawberry. When he was twelve months old, the pediatrician finally said it was OK to feed him berries, and so one morning I cut up a few at breakfast and placed them on the tray of his high chair.

Eamon grabbed a fistful of the ripe berries and put them into his mouth. Immediately, his eyes grew wide and he turned to me with a broad smile.

"Do you like those?" I smiled back at him. "Aren't they good?"

As fun as it was for me to watch him discover the joy of delicious fruit, the part that stood out and was most precious to me was that, in that small moment of joyful discovery, my son turned to me.

This is what babies do. They turn to us. In all the big and small moments, all the ins and outs of their tiny lives, they turn to us. Because no pleasure is ever complete until it is shared with their mom or their dad, the ones they love and trust the most.

I remember my dad joking years ago, when I called to tell my mother about an exciting new project I was working on, that for me, no experience could be considered "real" until I had told my mother about it. It was so true! My mom still plays that role in my life.

And so it should be with us. We too should find in every good thing, in every earthly pleasure, a natural nudge toward God, our Father and the Creator of it all. In every small thing we might ever enjoy, we should turn to God and smile.

But perhaps we can't start with how it *should* be. Maybe we need to begin where we are. Because where we are is sometimes so rushed and busy, we miss the joys God has planned for us. We rush through breakfast without tasting the strawberries.

Once, when my son Raphael was still very young, we spent a long day visiting friends and returned home after dark. It was a frigid January night, and so I bundled him in a blanket and carried him swiftly through the cold toward the house. I might have been in a hurry, but he certainly wasn't.

He gazed up at the sky and sighed. "Stars," he said dreamily.

I looked up. And took a breath.

Have you ever seen the sky on a clear January night in The Middle of Nowhere, New Hampshire? Thousands of brilliant white stars twinkled against a black velvet sky. I'm not sure I even knew there were that many stars. They winked and blinked and seemed almost to dance from where they hung in that enormous dome of black.

I hugged my bundled boy close, and the two of us spent a moment breathing the icy air and gazing through the darkness at the twinkling sky. I found it hard to believe that without my son's invitation, I would have entirely missed the enormous display of stunning beauty that hung overhead.

Thank you, God, I found myself praying, *for this glimpse of heaven, in my arms and in the sky. Thank you for the cold that makes us seek warmth. For the darkness that makes us seek light. And for small people who remind us to stop once in a while and look up. With wonder.*

We need reminders like these, don't we? A friend of mine, a working mother of four, recently told me of a time when she went to church but, once there, found herself so distracted and exhausted that she could not concentrate on praying.

"I can't even keep up with my everyday life," my friend sighed in the end. "How will I ever have a relationship with God if I have to chase him down first?"

What we don't realize when we are busy and distracted, though, is that we never have to chase God down. He's right here. Right here, right now. It's just that we sometimes need to peel back the layers of our lives that we have piled on top of God before we can recognize his presence.

Kids can be good at helping us do that. Their lives have fewer layers.

One night years ago, my then six-year-old Gabrielle got out of bed. She stood in the dark, at the foot of my bed, and did her very best to sound confident.

"I don't know why I can't sleep," she said. "But I just can't."

Her voice was tight and just a tiny bit trembling. In it, I heard more "I'm scared and alone in the dark" than my growing-up girl was prepared to admit.

I took her by the hand and led her back to her bed. I pulled up her covers and then knelt on the floor beside her.

"Let's talk about lovely things to think about as you are falling asleep," I said.

She began our list: Tiny fairies with flowers in their hair. Ice skating on a frozen lake. Ruffled pink skirts that twirl when you spin. Hot cocoa with candy canes. Angel wings. Easter eggs hiding in small patches of snow. Babies' first kisses. Cinnamon toast breakfast by the wood stove.

I was amazed at how easily a list of small joys seemed to come to her. My mind was more readily filled with grocery lists and phone calls to make and the laundry piling up in the boys' bedroom. Soon Gabby had no more suggestions, though, as her breathing grew slow and deep.

Even after she fell asleep, I remained there, listening to her steady breathing and adding to our list in my head. I spoke to God now and thanked him for the many blessings he has given us. *Every moment of our days should be as peaceful and pleasant as this one*, I thought to myself.

But then, I know that every moment truly is peaceful and pleasant, beneath the noise and commotion, under the clutter and the pressures of daily living. We need to slow down enough to dig deep, see that those moments are there, and treasure them for what they are—glimpses of God.

Our sensory experiences are an important part of how we learn about the world, and ultimately, a way that we can know God. Small pleasures of daily life are one thing, but some of us have a more complicated relationship with pleasure in a more general sense.

When I told my husband, Dan, I would be writing a chapter about finding God in pleasure, he cringed a bit and asked, "Are you going to talk about sex?"

So yes, let's talk about sex.

Do you remember the scene from the movie *Pinocchio* where Pinocchio is lured and tricked into taking a trip to Pleasure Island? I have to admit being scarred by more than one sinister Disney scene as a kid, and this was one of the worst. On the island, which looks like a giant amusement park, young boys are encouraged to smoke, drink, gamble, eat, fight, and break things.

"Go ahead, boys! It's all free!" an anonymous voice urges them on.

We soon find out that the pleasures of the island are not truly free, though, when Pinocchio's friend Lampwick undergoes a surprising physical change. Pinocchio watches in horror as his friend turns into a braying donkey, and then panics when he finds himself sprouting a donkey's tail and ears. The evil secret of Pleasure Island, we discover, is that it turns boys into donkeys. The boy-donkeys are then rounded up by an evil coachman who sells them into slavery. They are forever doomed to a beastly lifetime of manual labor as a result of chasing a few fleeting moments of pleasure.

There's a lot to unpack here, but the gist of the story holds true in young minds, and older ones too. Beware the power of pleasure. Diving too deeply into pleasure, whether it be from food, sex, money, or power, can strip you of your humanity and sell you into the slavery of sin.

I once read about a study where scientists in a lab gave rats a dose of sugar every time they performed specific tasks. If they tapped a wall, they got some sugar. If they completed a maze, they got some sugar. As they repeated and learned the patterns, the tasks became more complicated, but the rats kept up, motivated by the sugar high. Finally, the scientists made the required tasks painful. In order to get the sugar, the rats had to touch a wire that would deliver an electric shock to their bodies. And they did it! Over and over again, at increasing levels of intensity, the rats injured themselves in order to get their dose of sugar.

Of course we are talking about rats here, but how many of us read about a study like this one and pause because we recognize some of our own tendencies and behaviors in the ridiculous rodents? What pleasure in our lives might be like a rat's dose of sugar? What harm might we be willing to cause ourselves or others in order to get more of that high?

I wonder sometimes at the human capacity for destroying ourselves in pursuit of pleasure. Whether it's drugs, food, sex, wealth, or power, we humans have a way of taking things too far and perverting the good things God gives us.

I was with my brother David once when he rose from the couch after a long time sitting there, reading a book. He stretched extravagantly and sighed, "Ahhhh, licit pleasure!"

Licit pleasure. That's the key. What makes some pleasures licit and others not? Where is the line we should not cross?

One thing I think it's helpful to realize is that all pleasure we experience comes from God and is a reflection of God himself. All beauty is a reflection of the beauty of God. All goodness is a reflection of the goodness of God. Even when we pursue pleasure in evil or sinful ways, the experiences we desire are attractive to us because they reflect something beautiful and true. They are meant to point us toward God.

Pornography is a terrible sin and an affront to the dignity of every human being, and yet it is a multibillion-dollar, worldwide industry. Like rats in a maze, people pursue it. But what, exactly, are they pursuing? I think they are pursuing God.

Does that sound weird? I'll try to explain.

Whether he recognizes it or not, even an atheist experiences God and is drawn powerfully toward God through beauty and pleasure. A classic work of art might show us the female body in a way that is both beautiful and inspiring. In this way, human beauty can be an icon, something that turns our gaze toward the beauty of God.

In pornography, the beauty of the human body and the pleasure of sex are real, and yet they are twisted. They are twisted because they seek to replace God, the one we are made for, with the very things God himself created. The beauty of the human body is still real, and God is still the source of its attraction, but instead of being an icon, the human body becomes an idol, something we pursue as an end, an object, in itself.

We aren't made for food or sex or money. We are made for God. And that's how we can begin to see that line we should not cross. Failing to see good things as reflections of God, and instead seeking them in place of God, is always a perversion that robs us of our human dignity.

In Scripture we read, "So, whether you eat or drink, or whatever you do, do all to the glory of God" (1 Corinthians 10:31). We can enjoy all things properly when we seek God's glory first. This, I realize, should be my measure. If we seek God before all the other things, all the other things will fall into their proper places.

In fact, when I make efforts to see and experience God, even in the most mundane of sensory experiences, I know this to be true. The taste of a delicious meal, the warmth of sunshine on my skin, or the comfort of a soft bed are small joys that can turn my heart toward God, if I will allow it.

But do we allow it? How far have we allowed ourselves to move away from God? I heard a priest tell a funny story once about an old couple that pulled up next to a young couple at a stoplight. The young man was driving, and his wife was the passenger, snuggled up close, resting her head on his chest. The older couple observed this scene for a moment before the wife turned to her husband and said, "We used to be like that."

"Well," he replied. "I didn't move!"

God doesn't move either. If you find yourself thinking longingly of a time when God felt close, when you enjoyed knowing him and feeling his presence in all the moments of your day, it might be time to consider the ways in which you might have moved away.

Being busy is one way we move away. Have you noticed that we tend to wear "busy" like a badge of pride? We might run into an old friend at the post office and ask how she's been.

"How are you?"

"Busy! How about you?"

"Busy!"

We are so busy with all the "important" things we feel pressured to do, and we fail to see that our busyness distracts us from small ways we might experience God in the joys of daily living. We speed through dinner, scarcely tasting it, because we need to drive the kids to soccer. We miss the simple beauty of a sunny summer afternoon because our eyes are on our phone screens.

In our culture, it's easy to get caught up in a whirlwind of activity at school, at work, and even in our recreation, just because everyone else is signing up for swim lessons or staying late at work or running a half-marathon. We make ourselves busy for the sake of being busy. We send emails about things we don't care about and check off to-do lists of things we never actually wanted to do. The sad result is that we miss God himself, who waits for us inside every moment of every day, inside every small experience we ever have.

Can I go first and say let's stop? Can we pause?

Let's really feel and experience every small thing God has planned for us inside of this day. This day, right here, in our everyday homes, inside of our everyday routines, sharing meals and moments with our everyday friends and family.

Have you ever started to drink a glass of water and been startled to find yourself suddenly gulping because it was only when you started to drink that you noticed just how thirsty you were?

So many of us are walking around thirsty. In the Psalms, we read, "I stretch out my hands to you; my soul thirsts for you like a parched land" (Psalm 143:6).

We are parched. We are longing for God, whether we realize it or not. We need to pause more often and allow ourselves time to drink in the goodness that is God, a goodness we were made for, a goodness that is all around us, if only we will take it in.

One recent summer evening, I drove thirty minutes to a nearby field to watch my fifteen-year-old son Raphael's baseball game. And let me tell you something: God is in baseball.

God is in the glorious glowing green of the field under the lights. He's in the pastel-painted sky that stretches wide overhead as boys pitch and hit and run. He's in the sound of coaches' shouts, the umpire calling "Striiiiike!" and the thump of the ball as it hits the catcher's glove. God is in boys' man-sized bodies wearing dirt-stained uniforms that look like the ones men wore over a hundred years ago.

And God was there that night when, at the top of the sixth inning, fierce winds began to blow and the clouds opened up, soaking all of us with a sudden deluge of warm summer rain. Umps called the game, and there was a whoop of victory as players raced to cover the mound and fans scrambled to their cars.

Dan and I ran to our car together. I opened the passenger door and landed, breathless, in the front seat. Dan turned on the air conditioning to clear the windshield, and goosebumps covered my soaked arms and legs. Sheets of rain pounded the car. I looked ahead and saw Raphael, running toward us in the dark, pulling off his cap and grinning in the downpour. His smile was a striking flash of white beneath the lights.

I shivered and felt wonderfully alive. Fresh air filled my lungs, and my heart beat hard inside my chest. I felt loved, and in love—with my husband and my son and with the powerful beauty of the glorious world that God created that night just for us. I delighted in God, and in that moment, I felt God delighting in me.

"Take delight in the LORD, and he will give you the desires of your heart" (Psalm 37:4).

Teach me to delight in you, Lord. Help me to know
that every good thing comes from you. Every good thing,
from the food that we eat to the air that we breathe and the
love that we share, comes from you. You are the source
of all happiness and lasting joy, and you are always with us.
Thank you, God, for the gift of right here, right now. Amen.

CHAPTER THREE

Leaning In: Seeing God in Pain

I pressed my forehead against the wall and squeezed my eyes closed, but I could still hear her. She stood by my side and yammered on.

"I am *positive* that you would enjoy using the birthing ball. Studies show that it really helps women in labor to achieve positions and movements that reduce pain. Many of our patients choose to use the birthing ball, and I can just see the difference it makes for them. It actually increases their confidence. How about if I go get it for you? ... Danielle, would you like me to get the birthing ball?"

Helpless, I looked at my husband Dan, praying he could read my eyes, as yet another wave of pain rippled through my body.

"We don't want the birthing ball," Dan told the nurse.

This was my fourth experience of labor pain. I thought I would be a pro at managing childbirth by now, but I still remember those hours as among the worst of my life. The chatty nurse and her love of birthing balls was only part of the problem. The largest part of what made that experience so uncomfortable for me was that it was my first induced labor. I was attached to an IV that dripped

Pitocin into my arm. Every thirty minutes or so, the nurses would adjust the dosing, and my labor would intensify. I did not like watching them increase the dose, knowing what it would do to my body. Turns out, I prefer a healthy dose of ignorance and passivity when it comes to labor pain.

Hours later, as I held my perfect daughter Juliette, I marveled at the fact that a beautiful blessing can come from such a raw experience of pain. Pain is evil, right? It's something we should avoid at any cost, isn't it? At least that's what our culture will tell us: Have another drink, leave your husband, do anything at all to prevent suffering of any kind.

When we suffer in any way, it is normal to ask why. Why does this have to happen? Why would God allow this?

In some of our worst moments of suffering, it can feel not only like God is not present, but that he is very far away. We feel abandoned and betrayed. We get frustrated and angry.

I will never forget the bleakness of the time, years ago, when my infant son was diagnosed with cystic fibrosis, an incurable, life-threatening genetic illness. A few days afterward, we went to Mass together as a family. I knelt before the crucifix as I had always done, but found that this time I had no words to pray. I was surprised by how angry I felt. I was entirely overwhelmed with the feeling that God had let me down. Betrayed me.

Didn't God know that I was the praying kind? That I was the going-to-church kind? He had broken our unspoken agreement—the one where I do all the "right" things and I play by his rules, and he, in turn, never allows anything bad to happen to me or anyone I love.

Do you have this kind of agreement with God?

This kind of agreement can go on for many years, and it can all feel very nice. The problem comes when a really bad thing does happen, and we are left to make sense of the cruelty of a loving God who has allowed it. Back then, I was at a loss to understand it, and I stayed in that place for some time. Some people find themselves in that painful place of feeling abandoned and betrayed by God and they never do leave. They can never see anything but the stark reality of pain inside of their experience of grief or loss or trial.

But that is not what God wants for any of us. What we fail to see sometimes, when we are stuck inside the limited experience of our pain, is that every kind of suffering is an invitation from God.

Does that sound horrible? You may be suffering through something right now, something terribly painful and confusing, and those words might just make you want to throw this book into the nearest trash can. Thanks for the "invitation," God, but I am all set!

It is human to want to avoid pain, and it is also human to want to understand it before we can accept it. You can embrace labor pain because you know it will bring forth new life. You can accept the pain of an eight-mile run because you know it will make you stronger. You might accept the pain of healing after surgery because you know that, ultimately, it will make you well.

But what happens when we don't readily see a reason for our pain? I can look back at my own experience now, as a confused and frightened mother of a very sick little boy, and see that it was an invitation to let go of control and to trust in God. But it was hard to see that back then.

Let's talk about the invitation to let go. Because that's the step that needs to happen first. Do you like to be in control of your life? Actually, let me rephrase that: Do you like the illusion of being in control of your life? Because we all know it's true—everything can be humming along smoothly in our lives, but all it takes is one car accident, job loss, breakup, earthquake, or medical diagnosis for us to realize that we are not in control of anything at all. We never were. There are just some times in life when it's easier to pretend than others.

We get uncomfortable when it's hard to pretend, but that is also where we can begin to know who we are, and who God is.

Jesus tells us, *"I am the vine, you are the branches. He who abides in me, and I in him, he it is that bears much fruit, for apart from me you can do nothing"* (John 15:5).

Did you catch that? Apart from him, we can do nothing. Nothing! Jesus could not be more clear about who is, and who is not, in control of things. And yet, how many of us have read that familiar passage, even many times through the years, and failed to grasp its real meaning? We hold on to the notion that we are in control of our lives until something unpleasant forces us to reckon with the truth.

But do you want to know who you really are? Do you want to know who God is? I do. I struggle to do it, but there is real freedom in knowing and accepting the truth. A real relationship with God can only begin when we allow ourselves to see who he is. To do that, we must come to terms with the fact that we are not God ourselves. We must let go of the illusion of all control and learn to trust in God.

If I think about it, I realize that every sinful or harmful thing I might ever do is rooted in a failure to trust God. This has been true from the beginning. Consider Eve, the mother of us all, in that moment in the Garden when she committed the very first sin. The serpent who tricked her did not at first tempt her with the sight of ripe fruit. He did not begin by telling Eve how juicy and delicious the fruit from the forbidden tree would be. He began by planting doubts.

"He said to the woman, 'Did God say, "You shall not eat of any tree of the garden"?' And the woman said to the serpent, 'We may eat of the fruit of the trees of the garden; but God said, "You shall not eat of the fruit of the tree which is in the midst of the garden, neither shall you touch it, lest you die."' But the serpent said to the woman, 'You will not die. For God knows that when you eat of it your eyes will be opened, and you will be like God, knowing good and evil'" (Genesis 3:1-5).

The first lie that led to the first sin was that God cannot be trusted. God does not want good things for us, the serpent says, and he is keeping all the good things for himself. If we want good things, we must take them for ourselves.

Perhaps that lie rings true for you right now. Perhaps there is some part of your life where you are clinging to the illusion of control, afraid to let go for fear of what you will lose if you do. What is it? Your job, your marriage, your kids, your money? Perhaps you are afraid of what God, who cannot be trusted, will do if you let go. I know I often am. I need to check and then recheck this feeling in my own heart, time and time again.

I remember rocking my infant daughter, Gabrielle, in the dark hours of the morning, just weeks after she was born. I held her close, began to pray, and stopped short. I recalled how months earlier, a close friend's newborn son had died from SIDS. I had driven to her apartment to be with her that morning, arriving just moments after the ambulance and police had left. The two of us stood silently next to an empty bassinet for a moment before she turned to me with a vacant look.

"How? ... Why? ... I can't ..." she barely whispered.

Those words haunted me now as I held my precious new daughter.

"How ... Why ... I can't ..." I heard, I felt, and I prayed those words, over and over, as I wrestled with the idea that our children are not our own. Nothing is our own. Every moment, every good

thing we enjoy, from our jobs to our homes to our marriages to our children to our very own lives, is a gift from God that rests in his hands alone.

You will not die. You will be like God. These are Satan's words that speak straight into the weakness of our human hearts, and still today, we tend to believe them. We want to believe them. We want to trust only in ourselves. Because that is the one sure thing, right? And yet, no. God is the One Sure Thing.

Jesus knows we have this weakness, especially in the face of suffering, and so he gave us an example of trusting and accepting. God calls on us to trust in him, but he doesn't just talk. He acts. God went first.

Jesus was fully divine, but he was fully human too. When he prayed in Gethsemane, in the hours before his passion and death, he felt the very human inclination to reject pain and suffering.

"Then he said to them, 'My soul is very sorrowful, even to death; remain here, and watch with me.' And going a little farther he fell on his face and prayed, 'My Father, if it be possible, let this chalice pass from me; nevertheless, not as I will, but as you will'" (Matthew 26:38-39).

Not what I want, but what you want. These are hard words to pray. Well, actually they are easy to pray—many of us pray them all the time in the Lord's Prayer: *Thy will be done.* The hard part is to actually mean them.*

Like when I watched nurses increase my doses of Pitocin and braced myself for the pain, we all dislike the idea of sitting back and watching as something painful happens to us or to someone we love. It is only human to want to avoid pain. I take great comfort from the fact that even Jesus wanted to reject his pain. "Let this chalice pass from me," he prayed, and we can pray those words too. The challenge is to follow them with the rest of Jesus' prayer, the hard part: *Not my will but your will be done.*

It is never God's will that we suffer, but he does allow it sometimes because he can meet us in our pain. Through our suffering, God can bring about great things, if we will allow it. Through pain, we can come to know who we are and who God is. He meets us in our pain and invites us to let go of control and to trust in him.

If you are suffering through something hard right now, the very idea that God wants to meet you in your pain might make you angry.

A popular quote attributed to C.S. Lewis says, "We are not necessarily doubting that God will do the best for us; we are wondering how painful the best will turn out to be."

And isn't that exactly how it feels sometimes? We think we know better. We reject pain and don't realize that sometimes we reject the goodness of God along with it; we reject the invitation from God to meet him, to know him, and to see him through our suffering.

Sometimes it can be simple to see God's presence in our larger moments of pain, grief, and loss—those dramatic times when we have no choice but to relinquish control of our lives. We might survive a car accident and suddenly realize how nothing is guaranteed and that all of life can change in a split second. We might be diagnosed with a serious illness, and we are forced to reckon with the fact that we are completely dependent upon God for our very existence, every moment of every day. A loved one might die unexpectedly, and in our grief, we might find ourselves with nowhere to turn but to God himself. Of course it does not always work this way, but for many of us, God's presence is most palpable in life-changing, dramatic moments like these.

But what about other kinds of pain? What about those little things that hurt us, exhaust us, deplete us, or simply annoy us every day? What about little losses, small things that disappoint us, or ways we sometimes feel discouraged? Is God present in small kinds of pain as well?

I thought of this the other day when I looked into the kitchen sink and found my favorite coffee mug lying at the bottom of it, in pieces. Perhaps it had been placed there and other items had been recklessly stacked on top of it. Perhaps some child of mine had knocked it from the counter to the sink and had scarcely paused to note the damage before wandering into the next room to watch television. Or perhaps some teenager of mine had used it to mix acrylic paints while creating his artwork and then had dropped it carelessly into the sink.

Whatever the cause, the result was the same. My favorite coffee mug, the one in just the size and style I prefer, with the not-too-wide, not-too-narrow brim, and with the adorable image of Pusheen the Facebook cat on it, the one given to me by my dear friend Tiffany last Christmas, was in pieces at the bottom of the sink.

It's in moments like these that I can feel equal parts wounded and ridiculous. Seriously. It's a coffee mug. This is the definition of a get-over-yourself moment if ever there was one. There are people grieving the deaths of their children in this world, there are people who don't have a safe place to sleep, and there are people suffering through wars and every kind of unthinkable abuse. I can suffer a shattered coffee mug. I have only about 13,000 others in the pantry to replace it. I am going to be OK.

I hate to even admit that it hurts, and yet still it does. That stupid mug brought me some comfort and some joy, and I'm sad to lose it.

I like to think that Jonah knows how I feel. I laugh out loud every time I read the story of how he became attached to a plant. Truly, a plant. Have you read this story?

In the Bible, we read that when God asked Jonah to preach to and convert the people of Nineveh, Jonah resisted at first because he knew the people in that city were sinners, and he did not think they were deserving of God's mercy. Eventually, though, Jonah does as God asks and preaches to the people of Nineveh, warning them that unless they convert, God will destroy their city. And it works! The people convert in droves. They repent of their sins and amend their way of life. Even the king converts! Jonah's mission is a great success. Jonah, however, is still angry. He holds a grudge against the people of Nineveh and against God for showing them such great mercy.

And then comes the plant:

"And the LORD God appointed a plant, and made it come up over Jonah, that it might be a shade over his head, to save him from his discomfort. So Jonah was exceedingly glad because of the plant. But when dawn came up the next day, God appointed a worm which attacked the plant, so that it withered. When the sun rose, God appointed a sultry east wind, and the sun beat upon the head of Jonah so that he was faint; and he asked that he might die, and said, 'It is better for me to die than to live.' But God said to Jonah, 'Do you do well to be angry for the plant?' And he said, 'I do well to be angry, angry enough to die'" (Jonah 4:6-9).

Angry enough to die. What am I "angry enough to die" over? A passing comment that hurts my feelings? Piles of laundry? A work meeting that went badly? A broken coffee mug in the sink?

I find encouragement in the story of Jonah and his precious plant because it tells me that, when I am attached to small things, and when small, seemingly insignificant things hurt me, God knows all about it. He's right there, noticing me and seeing my pain, my sorrow, my loneliness, my anger, and my grief, however big or small they are.

In the big and in the small things, he sees me, and he asks, "Is it right for you to be angry?"

Sometimes it is right for me to be angry, and I need to be for a while yet. But always, however long it takes for me to get there, I must see that my goal, my happiness, my life rests in God alone. I must unclench my fingers that cling so tightly to my things, my people, my ways, and my will. Only then can I find peace, healing, and wholeness in him.

Teach me to let go, Lord. Come into all the places where I cling to control and relax my grip. Give me courage to turn everything I have, everything I love, and everything I am back to you who are Goodness and Mercy and Love itself. Show me where you sit, waiting to meet me, inside of all the big things and small things I suffer each day. Let me see you there. Amen.

CHAPTER FOUR

Letting Go: Discovering God in Contentment

Let it go. The thought occurred to me out of nowhere.

I don't regularly hear voices in my head, and this was not a voice, but the words of my sudden thought were clear: Let it go.

My oldest daughter and I were hiking in the woods together. There is a small hill near our house that leads about two miles up to a fire tower. Red Hill is a familiar one we have hiked many times through the years, beginning when the kids were small. We used to pack sandwiches in backpacks sometimes, strap the littlest babies to our bodies, and make the just-challenging-enough trek up the hill to enjoy lunch with a view.

On this late August day, however, my oldest daughter, Kateri, and I had made a plan to hike Red Hill with our small terrier, Mr. Potts, her favorite dog in the entire world. Kateri was working full-time now and had an apartment of her own nearby, but she still visited regularly and loved any chance to take Mr. Potts on an outdoor adventure.

But I was running late. I had forgotten that I needed to pick up Gabby, our youngest daughter, at a friend's house, and then by the time I returned home and met Kateri there, I wondered if it was too late to hike.

"It might get dark before we get back," I said, checking my phone for the time of sunset.

"Let's just go!" Kateri replied as she grabbed Mr. Potts' leash and headed toward the car. "If we leave right now, there's enough time."

My phone confirmed that this was true, and so we made the short drive to the trail. Aware of our impending time limits, we hiked up the hill at a swift pace without taking time to stop and rest as we usually do. I gasped for breath, mosquitoes buzzed in my ears, and I felt a trickle of sweat run down the back of my neck.

We made it to the top in record time and then enjoyed a brief stop, taking in the familiar view of nearby lakes and forest. We snapped some sweaty photos of ourselves with goofy grins on our faces as our shadows grew long and, behind us, the sun dropped lower in the sky.

The way down was fast. As it grew darker, we moved more quickly, taking long strides over rocks and roots. Excited to be almost running now, Mr. Potts pulled at his leash ahead of us, only occasionally slowing his pace, sniffing the air, and barking into the dark woods around us.

"Yikes, what is in there?" we laughed, and moved even faster, racing the sunset.

And that was when I tripped. My foot caught a root on the dimly lit trail and I fell forward, breaking my fall with my left hand and knee.

"Oh, no!" Kateri ran toward me. "Are you OK?"

I stood quickly and assessed the damage. I was OK. My knee was scraped a bit, and two of my fingers were throbbing, but I was OK.

"Yes, I'm fine," I said. "Let's keep moving."

As we continued down the trail, moving a bit more cautiously now, the throbbing in my fingers intensified. I tried looking at my hand again, but it was too dim to see clearly, and we needed to focus on getting to the car before dark.

And that was when I had the sudden thought: *Let it go.*

Let what go? I pondered the words for just a moment before I felt sure of their meaning. Inside of that small thought, I heard an invitation: Let it go. Let go of this pain. Give it to God.

I could feel my fingers swelling, so I pulled off my rings and slipped them into my pocket. *OK, Lord,* I thought, *I'll let this go.*

When at last we made it to the car, I sat in the driver's seat and paused for a moment to examine my hand under the light. Two of my fingers were bleeding a bit and the swelling was noticeable, but it truly was not a big deal.

As we drove home, I thought more about my sudden thought and the invitation I heard in it. The pain from my fall, minor though it was, felt like a secret I was being invited to keep with God. I felt God asking me to let it go, but also to keep it. Keep it between us.

When we arrived home and Kateri described the elegant moment of her mother's graceful fall to the rest of the family, Dan looked over my hand and knee and asked if I was OK. I told him I was, and then smiled and told him I was going to take a shower before making dinner.

I was OK. That was true. But I noticed something in that moment. I noticed that what I typically would have done is tell Dan that my fingers were really hurting. I would have shown him that I could not bend them all the way, and that they were swollen, and then I would have enjoyed the sympathy and attention my loving husband would have given me.

And the thing is: There is nothing wrong with that. It's normal and it's good for married couples to love and care for one another.

But inside of that small moment I felt an invitation from God to discover something. I felt that God was showing me a place that I usually seek comfort, and that instead, he was inviting me to seek comfort in him.

The next morning, my fingers were stiff and still noticeably swollen. Every time I felt the pain in my hand as I went about making breakfast, unloading the dishwasher, doing laundry, or typing, I found myself opening my mouth to tell someone about it. I wanted to complain to Dan about it. I caught myself beginning to tell my kids about it. And I realized something humbling: I don't normally suffer small things silently. I tend to tell everyone within earshot all about my every ache and pain.

Every time I felt compelled to complain about my hand that day, though, I remembered that I had already let it go. I had given it to God, and there was nothing left to talk about.

And so my eyes were opened to the fact that I am an attention seeker. Well, we all seek attention, don't we? We all seek reassurance that we are noticed and we are loved. That's just human nature.

Have you ever prayed the Litany of Humility? It's a short prayer, attributed to Rafael Merry del Val, and one that is sometimes hard for me to pray. On the day that I struggled to keep quiet about the pain in my hand, I thought of two particular lines from the Litany of Humility:

That others may be chosen and I set aside, Lord, grant me the grace to desire it.

That others may be praised and I go unnoticed, Lord, grant me the grace to desire it.

The fact that it is hard for me to pray words like these is telling. The struggle I felt not to complain that day was telling as well. I don't want to be set aside. I don't want to be unnoticed. Jesus, grant me the grace to desire it.

I think the sticking point for many of us about the Litany of Humility is that, in it, the things we are praying not to receive—notice, acceptance, praise, and love from others—are all good things. There's nothing wrong with being noticed, accepted, praised, and loved by others, but the trouble comes when we seek these things first, when we seek comfort in other things, in place of seeking God.

God is everything I need. God is enough. Why do I struggle to see that? God knows we want other things, and he actually promises to give us all of them if we will only seek him first. Jesus tells us:

"Your heavenly Father knows that you need them all. But seek first his kingdom and his righteousness, and all these things shall be yours as well" (Matthew 6:32-33).

I sometimes doubt that God will give me what I need. I think I know better, or I worry, at least subconsciously, that he will forget me. Do you do that?

My struggle to keep quiet about the minor pain in my hand that day led me to consider other ways that I tend to seek comfort in things other than God. I might have a bad day and decide to post a photo on social media to rack up some likes. I might turn on Netflix. Or eat some ice cream. Or pour a tall glass of wine. I've been known to combine all of these things into one epic evening of self-pity at the end of some especially hard days.

And again, there is nothing wrong with any of these things at the surface. What's disordered sometimes is our relationship with these things, and the importance we give them in our lives.

God doesn't tell us to seek comfort in worldly things. He tells us to seek comfort in him. He tells us not to seek approval from others, but instead to keep secrets with him.

"And when you fast, do not look dismal, like the hypocrites, for they disfigure their faces that their fasting may be seen by men. Truly, I say to you, they have their reward. But when you fast, anoint your

head and wash your face, that your fasting may not be seen by men but by your Father who is in secret; and your Father who sees in secret will reward you" (Matthew 6:16-18).

In secret. I like to ponder the meaning of that. God invites us to keep secrets with him. What other secrets can we keep?

Refraining from complaining about a small injury helped me to see that fasting from things, even from good things, helps us to see how attached we are to them and reminds us to seek God first in all things.

So let's talk a bit about fasting. Actual fasting. You know, from food. Fasting from food is what Jesus is referring to in the passage above, and so it's a secret God specifically invites us to share with him. That seems to warrant some attention.

There is a long history and tradition of fasting within the Church. Most of us are familiar with the obligation to fast on Ash Wednesday and Good Friday. For many years, as I had multiple pregnancies and nursed many babies, I was secretly glad to be exempt from the obligation to fast during Lent. Though the Church's rules about days of fasting are rather vague and actually not very demanding (eat one full meal and two smaller meals that together do not equal one full meal), fasting is something I always considered extremely difficult to do. Hunger seems like such a powerful drive—how could I possibly deny it?

And for the years when I was pregnant or nursing, that mindset made sense. My body truly was not my own. Other people needed it, and they needed my nutrition too. But more recently, I have had to admit that is no longer the case. I can safely do something as small as skipping a meal now and then; it was just a matter of deciding I was strong enough to do that.

So one Lent, I decided to try. Besides Ash Wednesday and Good Friday, I picked certain days of the week when I would wait until a certain time to eat. I kept a small notebook where I wrote down the names of people and situations I wanted to pray for, and I decided I would offer my fasts for these intentions. I started with a modest goal of skipping breakfast and not eating until lunchtime. By 11:00 that morning, I pretty much figured that all those fasting monks I read about in college were either insane or liars, and that I for sure was going to wither away and die.

Except I didn't die. I lived to fast another day. And then another. And before I knew it, fasting became something I could reasonably do, for even longer stretches of time.

Through fasting, I became aware that I previously had a habit of eating immediately, whenever I felt the slightest pang of hunger, and even many times when I didn't, just because food was there. The world tells us to seek immediate gratification, but the countercultural notion of fasting teaches us that we can wait. We don't need to fill ourselves continually with every fleeting, passing thing. We don't need a constant influx of pleasures, praise, or attention if we sustain ourselves in God.

In *Introduction to the Devout Life*, St. Frances de Sales writes, "Besides the ordinary effect of fasting in raising the mind, subduing the flesh, confirming goodness, and obtaining a heavenly reward, it is also a great matter to be able to control greediness, and to keep the sensual appetites and the whole body subject to the law of the Spirit" (3.23).

It seems right that fasting would subdue the flesh. Hunger is such a basic, instinctual drive that if we can subdue this one, we can gain the spiritual strength we need to subdue others. We are meant to control our physical passions through the use of our reason, and fasting is a practice of doing exactly that. Controlling hunger can strengthen the inner "muscle" we need to control other drives like anger, lust, greed, and pride.

Through fasting, I came to experience what I would call a calming of my inner self. My inner voice of "ME-ME-ME! Pay attention to MEEEEEE!" was quieted by the regular experience of denying myself instant physical gratification in this most basic way. I didn't immediately grow a halo, but I did notice that I felt quieter on the inside, even as I went about the noisy busyness of my day. I had a greater sense of inner peace and stillness when I was not constantly being "fed" by things other than God.

I remember one day in particular, I was recording some videos, working with a small camera crew at my place of work. These videos were part of a series of reflections we were creating for Lent. We adjusted the lights and connected the microphone, and then I gave a series of short talks that I had prepared. We had been filming for about twenty minutes when a young woman working one of the cameras suddenly interrupted.

"I'm so sorry," she said. "We'll have to start over. I forgot to turn the mic on."

Now I never would have gotten outwardly angry at someone who made a simple mistake like that, but previously, that circumstance would have caused me a great deal of inner turmoil.

It's hard to record video. You need to keep your energy levels up, and it's tricky to deliver lines you have prepared and yet have them come across in a natural way. I had just spent twenty minutes of considerable effort that was now lost and would need to be redone. It was a frustrating thing, to say the least.

At that moment, though, I was surprised to realize that I didn't feel discouraged at all. I felt untouched, almost completely unmoved by the situation, as if I were simply doing the next right thing. The next right thing happened to be repeating the difficult work I had just completed that was now lost.

It was fine. I was fine. All was well. Keeping secrets with God was changing me.

When it comes to keeping things with God, Mary offers us the greatest example. It used to frustrate me to notice how quiet she is in the Gospels. I wanted to see her do more things. I wanted to hear more from Mary, in her own voice, about what it was like to ride a donkey for miles while very pregnant, what it was like to give birth in a cold and dirty cave, surrounded by animals, and what it was like to hold the infant Jesus, God made man, in her arms.

But at the moment of Jesus' birth, Mary doesn't say anything at all. "Mary kept all these things," we read, "pondering them in her heart" (Luke 2:19).

She was treasuring beautiful and precious things in her heart and keeping them with God. But Mary did not just keep the good stuff with God. She kept the hard stuff with him too.

Years later, when Mary and Joseph lose track of twelve-year-old Jesus and then at last find him in the Temple, amazing all the teachers with his wisdom and knowledge, Mary is confused.

"When they saw him they were astonished; and his mother said to him, 'Son, why have you treated us so? Behold, your father and I have been looking for you anxiously.' And he said to them, 'How is it that you sought me? Did you not know that I must be in my Father's house?' And they did not understand the saying which he spoke to them" (Luke 2:48-50).

Imagine spending three days searching for your child "anxiously" only to find him and have him ask why you bothered to look for him at all. I think I knew a little bit of that kind of frustration the night one of my teenage sons returned home from the amusement park many hours later than he was supposed to because his friend's car had broken down.

"Why didn't you call and tell me where you were?" I shouted at him when he finally showed up.

"It wouldn't have gotten me home any earlier," he answered with a shrug.

I think my son was grounded for a week after that incident, but Mary didn't ground Jesus. In fact, she didn't say anything at all.

"And he went down with them and came to Nazareth, and was obedient to them; and his mother kept all these things in her heart" (Luke 2:51).

Here again, even in a moment of anxiety and uncertainty, Mary gives us the example of keeping secrets with God, treasuring them in her heart.

I want to do that too. I want to practice turning to God in all things, my big things and little things, my good things and bad things. I want to practice filling myself up with God instead of with passing things. I want to turn to God with all my wants and desires, and rest in the true contentment of knowing that I have enough, and I am enough, because I have him who is all things.

Help me to let go, Lord. Show me how to empty myself of all the things I am tempted to turn to in place of you. Tell me the secrets you want me to keep. Help me to see the good things that you will give me if only I will stop striving for everything else and allow you to fill me up. Amen.

CHAPTER FIVE

Slowing Down: Seeking God in Stillness

The pine floor pressed into my small knees, and they began to ache. I shifted my position where I knelt beside my bed, squeezed my eyes shut, and did my best to focus on the words of the prayer as my older sister led me.

"Hail Mary, full of grace ..."

I wriggled. I squirmed. And when it felt like we'd said a hundred Hail Marys, I dared open one eye, just a tiny bit, to check our progress on the beads in my hand. We were only a little more than halfway through! I stifled a sigh and opened both eyes now, turning my gaze to the pile of stuffed animals that covered the foot of my bed. There was Cocoa, my stuffed koala bear, and Ellie, my stuffed elephant. They stared back at me with unmoving eyes, and suddenly shamed, I returned my attention to the prayer card my sister had propped on the pillow in front of me.

There on the card stood Mary, her face radiant with beauty, with arms outstretched in greeting to the three small children who knelt before her. Fatima. This was a story I knew well. My mother had told us this story many times, and we had even been allowed to watch a movie about it once. Many years ago, Mary appeared six times to three Portuguese shepherd children—Lucia, Francisco, and Jacinta—encouraging them in virtue and giving them prophetic messages to share with the world.

Even as I struggled to focus, I thought of what my sister and I might look like from heaven—two sweet children, kneeling in prayer, honoring the Mother of God and asking for God's blessings. How could Mary resist? I wanted to see her. Surely she would show up here!

And yet she did not. Mary's image remained, wordless and still, on the prayer card before me. This was only one of many times in my life that I anticipated a miracle and wound up disappointed. How easy it would be to behave and believe, I have thought many times, if only Mary would show up and actually speak to us. If only God would fill the sky with thunder and lightning, giving us encouragement and direction, from a booming voice in the clouds.

If only.

It's been many years since my sister and I knelt beside our beds praying the Rosary, but in my grown-up prayer life, I still sometimes feel like that squirmy little girl on the inside. Stuffed animals may not distract me, but what to make for dinner does. That phone call I forgot to make, our plans for the weekend, and words from a conversation with a friend linger in my mind, threatening to pull me away from focus on God.

Years ago, I heard a podcast interview with a man who had written a book about meditation. The man did not even believe in God, and yet something in the words he spoke about the practice of meditation rang true for me.

"Our bodies and our minds need to do this," he said. "We are made for it."

Made for it. We are made for God. And yet it does not always feel like I am made for him when I sit in a quiet corner of the house, long before anyone else is awake, and close my eyes to pray. It feels more like a battle.

I yawn, I notice that the windowsills need dusting, and I check my phone to see how much time has passed before scolding myself and returning to the lines in my Bible or prayer book.

"Let them have coffee before meditation,"[1] Archbishop Fulton Sheen once wrote, and I am grateful for the reminder that to be human is to be needy.

And so I let myself have coffee. Sometimes that means actually brewing a cup and waking up a bit before I attempt to pray. But other times, "having coffee" simply means relaxing my grip on what I think my prayer time should look like and instead being open to what it is, where I am, and who I am right now.

I am not yet a saint. I may never hear God's voice booming from the sky. I might never levitate, bleed from my palms, or walk on water, but I can choose to read a few lines from the Bible right now and then sit in silence, waiting to hear what God is whispering to me in them.

One recent morning, I read about the miracle of the multiplication of loaves and fishes.

"And taking the five loaves and the two fish he looked up to heaven, and blessed, and broke and gave the loaves to the disciples, and the disciples gave them to the crowds. And they all ate and were satisfied. And they took up twelve baskets full of the broken pieces left over. And those who ate were about five thousand men, besides women and children" (Matthew 14:19-21).

I read the passage slowly and carefully. Then I read it again. Then I closed my eyes, shooed away distracting thoughts as they appeared, one after another, and I listened. I have read this story of Jesus' miracle of multiplication hundreds of times, and yet the two words that God whispered to me in that moment were ones I had never noticed before:

Broken pieces.

They took up what was left over of the broken pieces, and there were twelve baskets full. Broken pieces are what we bring to God. Broken pieces are what God makes miracles from. The broken pieces we bring to him may not be worth much, but in God's hands, they can feed multitudes.

I may not feel that I have much to offer God in prayer, but I do have broken pieces. I have broken pieces of good will, broken pieces of desire for God, broken pieces of longing to grow in holiness. I can bring my broken pieces to prayer, place them in God's hands, and wait to see what he will do.

Those two words stayed with me that day, long after my morning meditation was done. I unloaded the dishwasher, considered the broken pieces of my desire to serve my family, and I gave them to God. I opened my laptop to begin a particularly unstimulating work project, and I gave to God the broken pieces of my desire to do good.

The words returned to me once when a friend called me in tears, worried that her teenage son was making terrible choices and that her husband might lose his job. I had no solutions to offer her, but I had broken pieces of compassion, broken pieces of generosity, and broken pieces of wisdom gained from my own experiences. I gave them to God, and I asked him to turn them into whatever my friend needed most.

Sometimes my broken pieces are simply the desire I have to connect with God and hear what he has to say, in spite of my distractions. And so I give them to him. Sometimes my broken pieces are the will I have to see God as he lives and moves and breathes in the world. I give him this, and he multiplies it, sometimes by telling me more of his life story in the Gospel.

Remember the story where Jesus calms the storm at sea? I have always loved this one because it's a scene I can readily relate to.

"A great storm of wind arose, and the waves beat into the boat, so that the boat was already filling. But he was in the stern, asleep on the cushion; and they woke him and said to him, 'Teacher, do you not care if we perish?'" (Mark 4:37-38).

Isn't this exactly where we find ourselves sometimes? Alone and frightened in a tiny boat in a stormy sea, while God sleeps in the stern? In moments of worry and uncertainty, when our boats are "already filling," we want to find God where he sleeps and shake him awake. "Do you not care?" we want to shout at him. "Do you not care that we are perishing?"

So many of the frustrations I experience in prayer are connected to this idea of a sleeping God. I want to wake him up. Especially when I am in need, I want to see God and feel him, I want to touch him and hear him. I want him to appear on demand, reassure me in all my fears, and fix every problem I encounter. And yet he sleeps.

Why does God sleep? Why does he allow us to feel so alone in the stormy seas of life? Why must we squint and strain to see him?

I wonder if Jesus' disciples felt a little bit foolish that day, after panicking and waking up Jesus with their shouts, when he silenced the storm with only a few words.

"And he awoke and rebuked the wind, and said to the sea, 'Peace! Be still!' And the wind ceased, and there was a great calm. He said to them, 'Why are you afraid? Have you no faith?'" (Mark 4:39-40).

No matter how many times God wakes up and calms my storms, still I find myself answering him sheepishly: Yes, Lord, still I have no faith. Still I struggle to see you, trust you, and believe in you. Yet I give that struggle to God; it's my broken pieces.

Last year, I picked out my own birthday gift—something I really wanted, but that my family probably would not have thought to buy for me. It was a set of tiles featuring the mysteries of the Rosary that I could hang outdoors.

The tiles were made in Italy, so it took a few weeks before they arrived, and when they did, I kept them in the box for a few weeks more, as I was not sure yet where I wanted to hang them. I finally chose a spot on our wooded property, one that is dry and far enough away from the house to be quiet, but also close enough to be easy to access.

Then one Saturday, I took clippers, a bow saw, and a rake into the woods, and I got to work. I found three separate groups of trees that seemed suitable for the three sets of mysteries of the Rosary I had tiles for, and I cleared the spaces around them.

The work was much harder than I thought it would be. I clipped and raked and sawed. I hauled away branches, sticks, and leaves. Hours later, I emerged from the woods, sweaty, blistered, and mosquito-bitten, but victorious. I had hung the tiles, and the beginnings of my outdoor prayer space were in place.

It's still rough out there. There are still roots underfoot, stumps, and messy bits of branches and fallen trees. But there is stillness too. And quiet. I can meet a sleeping God there.

The first time I prayed in my woodsy spot, it was early in the morning. Sun shone through the trees, birds sang, and a gentle breeze rustled the leaves. It occurred to me that this is something we can do. We can create spaces in our lives where God can sleep, where he can stay, and we can choose to meet him there. We can clear away the mess and make space for him.

The space we create might be a path in the woods, a corner in the living room, or a chair in our bedroom. We can clear clutter and make room for God in our living spaces, and then, more importantly, in our hearts.

I think God sleeps sometimes because he wants to show us something. He wants to show us the importance of being quiet and sitting still. He wants to show us that quiet and stillness are good for us, and that we are made for it.

The words Jesus says when he wakes up and rebukes the storm speak straight into my heart sometimes: *Peace! Be still!* But when he speaks them to me, they sound less like a rebuke, and more like an invitation: *Come. Have peace. Be still. Don't you know that you were made for this?*

I can bring my broken pieces and respond. I can welcome God in and invite him to sleep in my heart, to stay with me, even after the prayer book is closed and the noise and activity of the day surround me. God, who is outside of time, who knows all about the storms, can sleep here in me.

"Abide in me, and I in you," Jesus encourages us (John 15:4), and we can do just that. We can simply be. We can do all the things or we can do none of the things, and all shall be well, as long as we abide together.

And that's the part I am working on—finding contentment in simply being, unmoved and unmoving, because I am rooted in the immovable God.

I sometimes lead retreats with groups of women where we focus on the stories of women in the Bible. Whenever I tell a crowd of women that we are going to discuss the familiar story of Mary and Martha, they always laugh and nudge one another. We women love this story because we see so much truth about ourselves in it. Most of us can relate to the busy and distracted Martha, failing to appreciate the importance of her sister's stillness. There sits Mary, peacefully poised, at the feet of Jesus. She gazes up at Jesus and listens to his every word. Mary has chosen the better part, Jesus explains to Martha and to us. We, the busy and distracted, are missing out.

What better part? The better part of not doing anything, of simply being with God.

Sometimes, it can feel like we need to earn our status with God. We must say many prayers and do many good works, and only then can we enjoy God's favor. But God tells us that we don't need to do enough—we *are* enough. We simply need to allow ourselves to be, as he made us. We simply need to sit in God's presence to see him, and allow ourselves to be seen.

Julian of Norwich, who lived in fourteenth-century England, was not just an everyday mystic; she was a real-deal mystic who received visions of God himself. She described these visions in a series of writings which became *Revelations of Divine Love*, the first book ever published in English by a woman.

In the past year, I have been spending some of my morning prayer times reading *Revelations of Divine Love*, and as always, I find myself wondering at the gift of receiving visions, such a sure consolation of the presence and love of God.

In one of her visions, Julian saw Jesus holding something:

"In this He shewed me a little thing, the quantity of an hazel-nut, in the palm of my hand; and it was as round as a ball. I looked thereupon with eye of my understanding, and thought: What may this be? *And it was answered generally thus:* It is all that is made. *I marvelled how it might last, for methought it might suddenly have fallen to naught for little[ness]. And I was answered in my understanding:* It lasteth, and ever shall [last] for that God loveth it. *And so All-thing hath the Being by the love of God.*

"In this Little Thing I saw three properties. The first is that God made it, the second is that God loveth it, the third, that God keepeth it."[2]

And this has become one of my returning thoughts through many difficult times. "All that is made" rests in the hand of God. It lasts and ever shall, for God loves it. God made it, God loves it, and God keeps it. God made me, God loves me, and God keeps me, too.

I need to remind myself of these things. Especially when life gets busy or I become stressed, I forget that all things rest in God's hands. It can be easy to feel like all things rest in my hands or weigh on my shoulders and I must do all the things to be worthy. Ironically, it's in busy or stressful times that we can feel like we don't have time for daily contemplation, and yet it is during those times that we need it most.

One recent Thursday, I woke up early with a feeling of dread. A full day lay ahead, much busier than usual. Many things just accidentally had been scheduled on top of one another, and though technically there seemed to be time for it all, there was little time for a pause between dozens of phone calls, meetings, appointments, and responsibilities to my work and my family. Surely, on a day like today, God would not mind if I skipped morning prayers or rushed through them quickly, eager to get a head start on a busy day?

And yet something in my heart invited me to sit that morning, to take all my cares and worries and place them intentionally into the hands of God. And so I did sit. At first, my anxious mind still flitted from one thought to the next, and my stomach still clenched at the worry of all there was to do. But I deliberately examined each thought, each worry, and gave it its place in that tiny ball in the palm of God's hand. These were my broken pieces that day.

In Psalm 46:10, God invites us to "be still, and know that I am God," and I realize that it is only when we are still that we can know God. It is only inside the context of our relationship with our Creator that we can fully become what we are. His creatures. His people. His.

We're made for it.

St. Alphonsus once said, "In meditation, God is sought after by a discursive effort; in contemplation there is no effort of this kind, as God has been found and is gazed at."[3]

I am aiming for that kind of gaze. I am beginning to understand that achieving that kind of gaze is less about finding God and more about allowing God to find me. Even as I go about doing many things, I want to be still inside, seated at the feet of the one who made me. I want to move beyond that discursive (or rambling) effort St. Alphonsus describes and find myself in the presence of God right now, right here, wherever I am.

I want to take all my worries, all my actions, all my must-dos every day. I want to gather them up and place them, like so many broken pieces, into the hands of him who is, who was, and who ever shall be, world without end.

Lord, help me to be still. Help me to see that all of the things
I have and all of the things I do are broken pieces that I can place
in your hands. I want to sit and gaze at you. Help me to see that
I have enough and I am enough only in you, the one who made me,
loves me, and keeps me every minute of every day. Amen.

CHAPTER SIX

Tuning In: Hearing God in Inspiration

Sometimes the Holy Spirit is on Facebook.

I squinted my eyes and zoomed in on the photo. It took me a minute to recognize who it was, but when I did, I paused. It was my then eight-year-old daughter Gabby with her arm around my friend Michelle's son, David, who could not have been older than three at the time. They were seated side by side in an armchair with a pile of storybooks on their laps. The two grinned at me widely from the computer screen, their faces filled with joy.

Facebook told me this was a "memory" from six years ago, but it felt so long ago and far away. I could not recall many other details from that day that my friend and I had gotten together at her house and our kids had enjoyed reading and playing together while we chatted in the kitchen.

Michelle was an old friend of mine from many years ago, but she had since moved across the country, and we had fallen out of touch. There wasn't a dramatic parting of ways, just the falling away from one another that happens when two friends' lives go in separate directions. She wasn't on social media, so I had not even seen a photo of her or her son since that day years ago. As my cursor hovered over the photo, I had a sudden, urgent thought: "I should call her!"

But then I realized it was early in the morning, and with time zone differences, Michelle would most definitely be asleep. I decided to text her a copy of the photo instead.

"Remember this? Missing you!" I typed, and sent it, smiling at the thought that hours later, she would wake up and know, first thing, that an old friend was thinking of her.

Almost immediately, though, three little dots appeared on my phone. Michelle was texting me back.

"Can you call?" she wrote. "I could really use someone to talk to right now."

She answered the phone with a shaky voice.

"We're getting a divorce," she told me. "I haven't told anyone yet. It's such a mess, and I have been just sitting here, crying all night, not knowing what to do. I couldn't believe it when I saw your text."

I couldn't believe it either. It was odd to think of how close Michelle and I had once been, that for years we had fallen almost completely out of touch, and now suddenly we found ourselves connected again in one of the hardest moments of her life. Just when she needed someone.

After I hung up with Michelle that day, I recalled the sudden, urgent thought I had to call her. I had no idea what she was going through. I had no idea she was awake on the other side of the country, feeling desperately lost and alone, but God knew. And he connected us.

When the Holy Spirit came upon the apostles at Pentecost, it was a dramatic and unmistakable moment.

"And suddenly a sound came from heaven like the rush of a mighty wind, and it filled all the house where they were sitting. And there appeared to them tongues as of fire, distributed and resting on each one of them. And they were all filled with the Holy Spirit and began to speak in other tongues, as the Spirit gave them utterance" (Acts 2:2-4).

I tend to prefer Biblical moments like these, when the presence of God is clear and indisputable. There's wind, there's fire, a beautiful dove might even appear in the sky. But the Holy Spirit does not usually appear like that to me. There's no fire, but there might be a sudden thought. There's no violent wind, but there might be the whispering of an idea. And the thing is, I need to be open to it and pay more attention; otherwise I might miss it altogether. I need to listen.

I once worked with a young woman who talked about her conversations with God as if he were her next-door neighbor. She would say things like, "During lunch today, I told the Lord that I was worried about my mother's upcoming doctor's appointment, but then he told me not to worry. All her tests will come back fine." Or "I was going to take the bus home, but the Lord told me that I should walk instead."

I don't doubt her sincerity, but that has never been my experience of God. I don't hear him the same way I might hear a friend, counseling me through my worries over lunch. I used to worry that meant I wasn't as holy as my coworker or others who experience God in such straightforward ways, and that may be so, but I need to accept who I am. I can work at being open to the subtle, more everyday ways God might speak to someone like me.

St. Faustina was a real mystic, a nun who lived in Poland during the early twentieth century. Throughout her life, she received many visions of Jesus. Those of us seeking connection with God would do well to listen to her, and that is blessedly easy to do as she faithfully wrote down her many thoughts and experiences in her diary.

In one passage, she tells us everyday mystics how we can work at hearing the voice of God:

"A noble and delicate soul ... sees God in everything, finds Him everywhere, and knows how to find Him in even the most hidden things. It finds all things important, it highly appreciates all things, it thanks God for all things, it draws profit for the soul from all things, and it gives all glory to God. ... It follows faithfully the faintest breath of the Holy Spirit; it rejoices in this Spiritual Guest and holds onto Him like a child to its mother. Where other souls come to a standstill and fear, this soul passes on without fear or difficulty."[4]

I want to see God in everything and find him everywhere. I want to hold onto him like a child to its mother. I want to follow faithfully the faintest breath of the Holy Spirit. The faintest breath! If I am too busy scrolling through Instagram, I might not notice the faintest breath. I need to pay attention.

The good news is that if we make a habit of paying attention, it gets easier to hear and be faithful to the voice of God in the everyday. St. Faustina also writes,

"O my Jesus, how very easy it is to become holy; all that is needed is a bit of good will. If Jesus sees this little bit of good will in the soul, He hurries to give Himself to the soul, and nothing can stop Him, neither shortcomings nor falls—absolutely nothing. Jesus is anxious to help that soul, and if it is faithful to this grace from God, it can very soon attain the highest holiness possible for a creature here on earth. God is very generous and does not deny His grace to anyone. Indeed He gives more than what we ask of Him. Faithfulness to the inspirations of the Holy Spirit—that is the shortest route."[5]

I'm not sure St. Faustina's definition of "easy to become holy" matches mine, but I can try, and I am encouraged to hear that neither my shortcomings nor my falls can get in God's way. All that is needed is a little bit of good will. I think I have that.

Even when we have good will, though, many of us worry about how we can discern what God is calling us to, what God wants, and how we can be sure it is his voice we are listening to, especially when it comes to making big decisions. Sometimes it can be easy to overthink it.

When I was a sophomore in high school, I enrolled in an honors English class with Mrs. Williams, a teacher who had a reputation for setting high standards and demanding excellence from her students. One of our first assignments in that class was to write a persuasive essay. On the day the essays were due, Mrs. Williams instructed each of us to spend our last few minutes of class going through our work and clearly marking our thesis statements and supporting paragraphs before turning it in.

I panicked. I knew the definitions of "thesis statement" and "supporting paragraphs," but I had not even thought about adding any of these to my paper. I had just written an essay about why the voting age should not be changed to twenty-one.

I flipped anxiously through the pages of my essay for a few dreadful minutes and finally wrote a note to Mrs. Williams in the margin. "I'm sorry," I wrote. "I do not have a thesis statement."

I turned the paper in and went home with a knot in my stomach.

The next day, Mrs. Williams asked me to stay after class. She pulled my essay from her briefcase, and I saw that it had been marked with red ink.

"This right here?" she said, pointing to two underlined sentences. "This is your thesis statement."

"And these here?" she said, pointing out several other marked parts of the paper. "These are your supporting paragraphs."

"You can write," she told me. "Don't overthink it."

Don't overthink it. It would be helpful if God's messages to us were underlined in red pen so that we might not miss them. Straining to hear the tiniest whisper or struggling to feel the faintest breath, though, we might miss some of the large and loud ways that God sometimes speaks to us.

Years ago, a young woman I knew asked me how I "discerned" that I was called to be married, how I "discerned" that it was Dan I should marry, and how we "discerned" when we should get married.

I had no answer for her because it didn't feel like I "discerned" those things at all. Dan and I were just crazy about each other. We could not wait to get married and start a family together. We were in a wild hurry to start being "together forever," whatever that meant, and I have no doubt that was God's will for us.

Sometimes we make things more complicated than they need to be. God can speak his will to us through tiny whispers, but he also communicates his will through those things we love, what we are passionate about, and the desires for good things that he places in our hearts. If you are a skilled teacher and you have a passion for teaching, it takes very little "discernment" to decide to become a teacher.

Have you read *In the School of the Holy Spirit* by Fr. Jacques Philippe? If not, just toss this book back on the shelf and go get yourself a copy right now. It will change your life. It's that good.

In it, Fr. Philippe outlines some of the most basic ways that the Holy Spirit speaks to us, pointing out that very often, doing the next right thing, the next logical thing, is what God does indeed want for us. He says this with the caveat, of course, that God never calls us to something that contradicts his commandments, the teachings of the Church, our current state in life, or counsel from trusted people who have legitimate authority over us.

Often, it is just that simple. But what about times when it is not? What can we do to hear more clearly the small ways God might call us to grow in holiness, every moment of every day? One of the easiest ways that Fr. Philippe recommends is simply to ask for the inspirations of the Holy Spirit:

"We must, of course, desire God's inspirations and ask for them frequently in prayer: 'Ask, and it will be given you.' One of the petitions we make to God most often should be: 'Inspire me in all my decisions, and never let me neglect any of your inspirations.'"[6]

And so I ask. Before I open my Bible each morning, I ask God to help me hear his voice in what I am about to read. Before I attend a meeting, record a podcast, or call a friend, I ask God to inspire me with the words I should say. I'm not perfectly consistent at it, and for sure I'm not setting world policy in my little work here in my little family in my little home in New Hampshire, but I want to be open. I want to hear every little next right thing God might call me to.

St. Thérèse of Lisieux wanted that too. In her autobiography, *The Story of a Soul*, she writes,

"I understand and I know from experience that: 'The kingdom of God is within you.' Jesus has no need of books or teachers to instruct souls; He teaches without the noise of words. Never have I heard Him speak, but I feel that He is within me at each moment; He is guiding and inspiring me with what I must say and do. I find just when I need them certain lights that I had not seen until then, and it isn't most frequently during my hours of prayer that these are most abundant but rather in the midst of my daily occupations."[7]

I find encouragement in the fact that even a spiritual giant and Doctor of the Church, St. Thérèse, never heard God speak directly. She "heard" him through small inspirations in her everyday life, and she was careful to respond to them.

I think I can do that. And when I work at asking, listening, and responding to even small inspirations from God, my efforts sometimes bear fruit in striking ways.

I recently read the passage from Matthew where Jesus teaches Peter about forgiveness.

"Then Peter came up and said to him, 'Lord, how often shall my brother sin against me, and I forgive him? As many as seven times?' Jesus said to him, 'I do not say to you seven times, but seventy times seven'" (Matthew 18:21-22).

I reflected on these words for a while, considering the infinite number implied by the number seven as Jesus uses it here, and feeling the daunting task God sets before us to forgive others always. And then I moved on to other things. Days later, though, the words from that passage came back to me.

Dan and I had gotten on each other's nerves that morning. There was a misunderstanding between us, and, though it was not a big deal and he probably didn't even mean to, he said something that hurt my feelings. A short while later, we were both standing in the kitchen when I decided I needed to let him know just how inconsiderate I thought he was.

I opened my mouth to speak, but then hesitated. I was struck by the sudden thought that I should tell Dan I was grateful for him instead. I resisted the thought because, in my great maturity, I still wanted to be mad. I wanted to be sure he knew all about my negative feelings.

But in that very moment, I recalled the words I had read from Jesus in the Gospel just a few days before, and they spoke loud and clear straight into my heart: *seventy times seven.* How many times must we forgive, Lord? *Seventy times seven.* And here I was, resisting one time in hundreds of days in a very happy marriage. There was no getting around it.

"I'm grateful for you," I told Dan.

He dropped his toast and turned to me with one raised eyebrow.

"Why are you saying that?" he asked.

"I just am grateful," I told him, "and I felt like I should tell you that."

He smiled. We hugged. It really was as simple as that. And yet, for me, it was life changing because it opened my eyes, opened my ears, opened my heart to the voice of God as something real. Something that I can hear and respond to. Something that I can nurture and that will bless my marriage, my family, my work, and my relationship with every human being I ever meet. One small moment, one tiny inspiration at a time.

What struck me most about that surprising moment in the kitchen that day was that the thought of those words—*seventy times seven*—stood out to me among the thousands of thoughts I might have on any given day. I did not hear them through my ears, but I felt them in my heart. Fr. Philippe writes,

"The Holy Spirit uses, for each of us, a 'tone of voice' that is his alone. It has particular gentleness and power, purity and clarity, which, when we are accustomed to hearing it, gives us near-certainty in singling it out."[8]

Near-certainty. I'll take it. And when I find myself faltering, I have the certainty of Jesus' own words to reassure me:

"And I will ask the Father, and he will give you another Counselor, to be with you forever, even the Spirit of truth, whom the world cannot receive, because it neither sees him nor knows him; you know him, for he dwells with you, and will be in you" (John 14:16-17).

Jesus loves us so much that, though he knows he must leave, he does not leave us alone. He promises to send us an Advocate, a helper, to be with us forever. He promises that he will be present with us and in us. And so he is.

*Come, Holy Spirit. Abide with me. I want to hear your voice
and do your will in all things, every moment of every day.
Speak your will into my heart, one little nudge, one little word
at a time, and give me the grace to heed it well. Amen.*

CHAPTER SEVEN

Journeying On: Meeting God in Prayer

I never should have said yes to the Airbnb.

When I was scheduled to give a retreat at a small parish in a rural area of Ohio a few years ago, the host texted ahead of time to suggest I might be more comfortable in an Airbnb instead of a hotel. It was right near the church where I would be speaking, she explained, and it was an apartment where I would have plenty of space.

I have stayed at many Airbnbs without problems, and so it seemed like a good idea to me. "Sure!" I texted back, and then forgot all about it.

Until the moment I was checking in. The nice lady who had picked me up at the airport helped me unlock the door, and the two of us stepped into the kitchen. She glanced around and grimaced. The place seemed clean enough, but it was ... I don't know, quirky? Perhaps that is how a realtor would describe it.

Instead of a coat rack, a large pair of antlers hung on the wall near the front door. The kitchen cabinets were painted a dark orange, and the countertops were covered in small, glossy tiles, a mixture of deep reds, browns, greens, and yellows. A hodgepodge of pots, pans, dishes, and baking ingredients were crammed on open shelves. The small living room offered an assortment of furniture pieces—an avocado green, varnished 1970s coffee table here, a long-past-its-prime college dorm beanbag chair there.

"It will be fine!" I told my ride, who was dubiously examining a dusty stack of records piled high on a stool in the corner. "I'm only going to sleep here."

She really wanted to drive me to a hotel, but I told her I would call if I had any problems, and I was sure that I would not. After she left, I carried my bag down the short hallway toward the bedroom and discovered the pièce de résistance: There was an enormous mural painted on the wall. It was a desert scene featuring a large cowboy with a ten-gallon hat, bolero, chaps, and boots with spurs. He was holding a rope above his head, twirling it into a lasso. His eyes squinted at me, and his mouth was a menacing scowl. This cowboy had not been painted by a particularly talented artist.

I took photos of the cowboy and the horseshoe light switches I found in the bathroom and texted them to my sisters and a couple of friends. My exotic trip to Ohio was too good not to be shared.

It was a weird place, to be sure, but I truly am not a fussy guest. It was late, and I was tired from traveling anyway, and so I turned on a cactus lamp in the living room to read for a little while before getting ready for bed.

When I woke up hours later, it took me a few minutes to remember where I was. I checked my phone: 3:00 AM. I turned over and lay in the quiet, dark room with an uneasy feeling.

Perhaps it was the drug addiction that I knew was rampant in the community where I was staying. Perhaps it was the story of a recent murder that had taken place in a nearby town that the nice lady had told me about on the ride from the airport. Perhaps it was the abandoned and graffiti-covered shell of a restaurant that I knew was next door. It probably was a combination of all of these things, but whatever the cause, I felt a heavy sense of evil and dread as I lay there in that room.

Now, I'm not the kind of person who goes around feeling the presence of evil. I try to be an everyday mystic, not the extrasensory kind. But the gloom in that place pressed upon me, and in a way I have not experienced since I was a little girl, I felt frightened there, alone in the dark.

I was born and raised Catholic, and so of course I prayed the St. Michael prayer. I repeated it a few times out loud, focusing on the words "by the power of God." Then I rifled through my bag, which was on a chair near the bed, and found my rosary. I pulled it out and began to pray a Divine Mercy Chaplet. It was 3:00 after all, the hour of mercy.

Eternal Father, I offer you the Body and Blood, Soul and Divinity of your dearly beloved Son, our Lord Jesus Christ, in atonement for our sins and those of the whole world.

As I repeated the familiar words of the chaplet, I was especially comforted by the power of saying out loud Jesus' name, and so when I was done, I continued to pray, saying only God's name now: "Lord Jesus Christ. Lord Jesus Christ. Jesus ... Jesus ... Jesus."

I eventually fell back asleep, and nothing more happened that night, but the experience reminded me not only of the comforting power of repetitive prayer, but also of a practice I used to have of regularly praying with the name of Jesus. A priest had recommended it to me in confession once. He explained that speaking Jesus' name out loud is a powerful practice, and we should pray his name often, especially when tempted to sin. There is a moment right before we might make the choice to do something wrong, he explained, and in that moment, we should say Jesus' name out loud and call upon the power of God to help us to choose good over evil. "The devil flees at the sound of Jesus' name," he told me.

Repeating the name of Jesus is a prayer practice with a long tradition in the Church. I have long been familiar with the practice of saying short prayers, or aspirations, throughout the day. My mother taught me years ago that repeating small prayers like "Sacred Heart of Jesus, I trust in you" or "Blessed be the name of the Lord!" can be a simple but powerful way to stay connected to God and pray throughout the day.

The Jesus Prayer is a practice like this, with an even deeper tradition, but not everyone is familiar with it. I first heard of the Jesus Prayer just a few years ago when I was working on a freelance writing project, creating a small booklet that would feature a collection of favorite Catholic prayer devotions. I decided to do some research the modern way, on Twitter, where I asked people to share their favorite devotions.

Some of the responses I got were familiar and predictable: the Sacred Heart of Jesus, the Rosary, and the Angelus. But then I saw a response that I did not recognize: the Jesus Prayer. They never taught me that one in CCD.

It turns out that the Jesus Prayer has a long history in the Eastern Orthodox Church. In practice, it's quite simple. Using a prayer rope with one hundred knots (or you can use a rosary if you're a Roman Catholic like me and that's what you have in your bag), you simply pray the following short prayer, over and over again: *Lord Jesus Christ, son of God, have mercy on me, a sinner.*

There are a few different versions of the prayer, some of them longer, and one of them as short as simply, *Jesus, have mercy.* It's meant to be a meditative prayer that can call you into a greater stillness and awareness of the presence of God. It's also meant to be a prayer you can take with you into every moment of the day, long after your meditation is done.

In my quest to learn more about the Jesus Prayer, I came across *The Way of a Pilgrim*, a spiritual classic in the Russian Orthodox tradition, written from the point of view of a young man in mid-nineteenth-century Russia. In the book, the young man, whose identity we do not know for certain, reads the urging of St. Paul to pray without ceasing:

"Rejoice always, pray without ceasing, give thanks in all circumstances; for this is the will of God in Christ Jesus for you" (1 Thessalonians 5:16-18).

The young man is troubled by this. He wonders what St. Paul can mean by instructing us to "pray without ceasing." Pray without ceasing? He wonders if it is even possible to do.

I must admit, I had read these words in the Bible many times before and was not especially troubled by them myself. I mean, St. Paul must be exaggerating for dramatic effect, right? Who, besides possibly a monk in a monastery or a nun locked away in a cloister, could possibly pray without ceasing? I would like to pray without ceasing, Lord, but I have kids to pick up at basketball practice and laundry that needs to be switched over from the washer to the dryer.

The young man in *The Way of a Pilgrim*, however, learns the practice of the Jesus Prayer from a wise old monk who instructs him to pray it three thousand times a day, then six thousand times a day, and then twelve thousand times a day. In the end, the repetition of the prayer, which at first felt like an arduous task, becomes a joyful practice, a continued, constant prayer experience that the young man longs for.

"My only desire was to go on with the Jesus Prayer, and no sooner had I started it than I felt joyfully relieved. My lips and my tongue recited the words without any effort on my part. I spent the whole day experiencing great happiness and a complete detachment from earthly things, as though I were living on another planet. Easily did I finish my twelve thousand prayers by the early evening. I wished I might keep on, but I dared not to increase the number fixed by my elder."[9]

As the young man wanders on, meeting new people and visiting new places along the way, he continues his practice of praying the

Jesus Prayer, growing more and more attached to it spiritually, emotionally, and even physically. In fact, many teach that one of the goals of the Jesus Prayer is to have it become part of your physical experience, by breathing in the words "Lord Jesus Christ, Son of God" and breathing out the words "have mercy on me, a sinner."

I am not a Russian pilgrim, and for a while yet, I still will have kids to pick up and laundry to attend to, but I decided to try the Jesus Prayer myself. I began by reciting it during a few moments of quiet in the morning and then tried to continue praying it, as a running refrain, in many other moments of my day.

Have you ever found yourself mindlessly humming a commercial jingle and then wondered just how long you had been allowing that drivel to run through your brain? I do this all the time. Like a good neighbor, State Farm is there! Not the best use of my brain space. Instead, I set a small goal of filling my idle mind moments with the Jesus Prayer. The simplicity of the prayer allowed me to jump right in and give "unceasing prayer" a try.

I would drive the kids to school, note the beauty of sunlight as it danced on the ripples of the nearby lake, and pray the words as praise: *Lord Jesus Christ, Son of God, have mercy on me, a sinner.*

I would find myself feeling stressed by a long list of to-dos and a looming deadline, and pray the words as a petition for God's grace: *Lord Jesus Christ, Son of God, have mercy on me, a sinner.*

I would give way to impatience, snap at my husband over something trivial, and then tell him "I'm sorry" before praying the words as an act of contrition: *Lord Jesus Christ, Son of God, have mercy on me, a sinner.*

In my mind, the words of the prayer became two parts: The first part called on the power of God and brought the presence of God to the forefront of my mind: *Lord Jesus Christ, Son of God.* The second part recognized my own weakness and surrendered myself to God's mercy: *have mercy on me, a sinner.*

Breathing in, breathing out.

It's not perfect, and it's not unceasing, but it is more than I was doing before, and I like to recall that, with his parables and example, Jesus himself teaches us to pray in this simple way. At first glance in the Gospels, though, it may look like the Jesus Prayer is exactly the kind of prayer Jesus tells us not to practice:

"In praying do not heap up empty phrases as the Gentiles do; for they think that they will be heard for their many words" (Matthew 6:7).

When prayed in the right way, though, the words of the Jesus Prayer are not empty phrases at all. They are a simple and yet deep prayer, rich with meaning. The parable Jesus tells about the Pharisee and tax collector exemplifies this. First, we meet the Pharisee as he prays his many words, giving thanks to God for his own good deeds.

"The Pharisee stood and prayed thus with himself, 'God, I thank you that I am not like other men, extortioners, unjust, adulterers, or even like this tax collector. I fast twice a week, I give tithes of all that I get'" (Luke 18:11-12).

A sinful man, standing at the back, however, prays differently:

"But the tax collector, standing far off, would not even lift up his eyes to heaven, but beat his breast, saying, 'God, be merciful to me a sinner!'" (Luke 18:13).

And Jesus explains that this humble, honest, simple prayer is the kind that God prefers:

"I tell you, this man went down to his house justified rather than the other; for every one who exalts himself will be humbled, but he who humbles himself will be exalted" (Luke 18:14).

Have mercy on me, a sinner. Humble words, sincere words, repeated again and again. This is how Jesus tells us to pray, and these simple words are rich with meaning. Even when we are not praying, we can recognize that there are some feelings and sentiments so deep and meaningful that we cannot adequately express them in words.

"I'm sorry," we might say when we have hurt someone we love, knowing that the words are woefully inadequate for how contrite we feel.

"Thank you," we might repeat many times, never feeling like we have expressed the fullness of our gratitude for someone else's extraordinary generosity or kindness.

And "I love you," we say every day to our friends, our spouses, our parents, and our children, but the mere words can never fully express all that we really mean by them.

The Jesus Prayer is like all these simple and yet inadequate phrases wrapped into one. *I'm sorry, thank you, I love you,* we say, over and over again. They're not empty phrases heaped up; they're sincere prayers repeated over and over again, with a simple trust that God will understand their meaning.

I once heard the repetition of prayers of the Rosary described as the pleas of a small child who pulls on her mother's skirt: "Mama, Mama, Mama," we pray to our mother in heaven with each Hail Mary.

So too, the Jesus prayer is a simple crying out to God, one that we know he hears, just as he heard the simple plea of Bartimaeus, the blind man who once sat waiting for him at the side of the road:

"As he was leaving Jericho with his disciples and a great multitude, Bartimaeus, a blind beggar, the son of Timaeus, was sitting by the roadside. And when he heard that it was Jesus of Nazareth, he began to cry out and say, 'Jesus, Son of David, have mercy on me!'" (Mark 10:46-47).

A simple plea that gets Jesus' attention. Many try to reprimand Bartimaeus and quiet him, but still he cries out, and Jesus is moved by his plea. He has Bartimaeus brought to him:

*"Jesus said to him, 'Go your way; your faith has made you well.'
And immediately he received his sight and followed him on the way"*
(Mark 10:52).

Bartimaeus' words are the same as the ones prayed by the tax
collector at the back of the church, and the same ones we repeat
in the Jesus Prayer: *Jesus, have mercy on me.* A simple, sincere
prayer, repeated again and again.

In the repetition of the prayer, I find a reminder of my own repeated
need willfully to turn my heart and mind toward God. Even when
I sit to pray, my mind might wander away from God and toward
other, more practical or frivolous things. Again and again, I need to
bring my mind back to God. In life, I might be tempted away from
God by a thousand worldly things, treasures and pleasures, wealth
and human status. "Unceasing" prayer reminds me that I am weak,
and until heaven I know I will never cease needing to interrupt
myself and turn my heart once again toward God.

I love the word "metanoia." Although it's a Greek word that seems
like it should be the name of a new pharmaceutical, it's really a
word for spiritual conversion. It comes from a Greek term for
changing your mind. A change of mind. A change of ourselves.
Repentance. We need an unceasing interruption that prompts us
to cry out to God, to turn our hearts toward God. Metanoia. Again
and again, it's what life is.

And we are not alone in our need for change, in our yearning,
longing, and crying out for God. All of creation joins us in this
prayer of longing for the fullness of life in God, our Creator.

*"For the creation waits with eager longing for the revealing of the
sons of God; for the creation was subjected to futility, not of its own
will but by the will of him who subjected it in hope; because the
creation itself will be set free from its bondage to decay and obtain
the glorious liberty of the children of God"* (Romans 8:19-21).

One recent early spring morning, I went for a run on the trails in
the woods nearby, and I brought the Jesus Prayer with me. As my

feet pounded the path, I prayed those ancient words I have prayed thousands of times now. Words I am still making my own:

Lord Jesus Christ, Son of God, have mercy on me, a sinner. Lord Jesus Christ, Son of God, have mercy on me, a sinner ...

In these words, I acknowledge my place in the world, and God's place too. And I see the place of all creation, all things that are reaching and praising and stretching toward God along with me. Beside the path, trees stand at attention, their dewy, green-leafed branches waving and dancing in the breeze. Sunshine filters through their leaves and falls in dappled patterns on the earth beneath my feet. Birds sing nearby, and frogs peep from thawing ponds as my sneakers crash through roots and brambles and stubborn patches of snow.

My lungs fill with fresh, cold air, in and then out again, and I know each breath as a gift from God. My heart pounds in my chest, and I know each heartbeat originates in God's will alone. He wills it, he thinks it, he loves, and I am. Thanks be to God, I am.

Over and over again, I pray the words, I breathe the air, and I return to God, recalling what St. Paul writes in Romans: *"We know that the whole creation has been groaning with labor pains together until now; and not only the creation, but we ourselves, who have the first fruits of the Spirit, groan inwardly as we wait for adoption as sons, the redemption of our bodies"* (Romans 8:22-23).

With St. Paul, with the tax collector, with Bartimaeus, and with all of creation, I cry out: Have mercy, Lord. We are waiting, Lord. Come, Lord Jesus, come!

Come, Lord Jesus, and hear my prayer. Accept the simple words that burst from my heart toward you. Praise, thanks, sorrow, petition, and love. None of them are enough, and yet I know that you will accept them as I pray and seek to love you more. Lord Jesus Christ, Son of God, have mercy on me, a sinner. Amen.

CHAPTER EIGHT

With the Help of Thy Grace: Everyday Confession

"How about right now?"

The priest's suggestion caught me off guard. It was early in the morning, and I had just arrived at a church conference hall for an event where I would be speaking.

When I saw the priest enter the building, I had decided to ask if he could hear my confession later that day. It can be hard enough making time to get to confession, but with my recent schedule of traveling every weekend, I knew that I needed to seize any opportunity that came my way. I thought that asking for a confession appointment later in the day was bold and brave enough, but here was something braver still: right now.

Father was smiling at me, awaiting my response. "Uhh, OK," I stammered.

He gestured toward some chairs in the corner. "I'll meet you right over there."

I sat in one of the chairs and struggled to focus my mind. So much busyness. So many distractions. So much to do and so many things to worry about.

I managed to make it through my confession, and at the end, when the priest asked me to recite an Act of Contrition, I began the familiar prayer I have known since I was a little girl. "Oh my God, I am heartily sorry for having offended thee ..."

I was still so distracted, though, that at one point in the prayer, my mind went completely blank. Have you ever done this? This is why, years ago, my parents taught me to bring a written list of what I wanted to say and a prayer card with the Act of Contrition on it into the confessional with me. Because nerves can make you stupid.

"I firmly resolve ..." I prayed, and I stopped. I could not remember the next line. "I firmly resolve ..." I tried again, but nothing. The next words, words that I have prayed thousands of times over the years, evaporated from my mind.

After a long pause, the priest prompted me, "With the help of thy grace ..."

Of course! With the help of thy grace! I completed the prayer. Afterward, however, as I reflected on my stress-induced lapse of memory, I recognized something significant in the words I had forgotten.

With the help of thy grace. I do all things with the help of his grace. In the midst of life's busyness, though, I can forget that. Instead of relying on God's grace, I believe lies. I believe that I am in control, that I can do all the things, and that everything and everyone is counting on me and me alone.

Without Jesus, though, the real Jesus I met in confession that day, the real Jesus we meet in confession every time we receive the sacrament, I am powerless. Every good thing I might ever accomplish comes from him and through him. He is the source of all that I need, and I can do nothing without the help of his grace. I can't love my husband or take care of my kids or speak at a conference. Nothing.

I know these truths in my head, but I don't always let them seep into my heart. I forget to rely on the help of his grace. Instead, I rely on myself as I fill my life with activity and distraction, as I worry about my family, friends, work, money, and health. I'm grateful for the priest's prompting that day to remember: *with the help of thy grace.*

It's also easy to forget that it's truly Jesus we meet in the sacraments.

"Are you sure you're all set?" I fussed at my youngest son, Danny, on the day of his first confession.

"Yes, I'm OK." Danny rolled his eyes, but I could see his smile was tense.

"Are you nervous? Don't be nervous! It's Jesus you'll be meeting in there," I continued. "And I'll be right out here, praying for you the whole time."

I watched as he waited in line among the other second graders. He shifted the weight of his small body from one foot to the other and fidgeted with the collar of his shirt. When at last it was his turn, I watched as he entered the confessional and closed the door. Then, in the silence of the church, I knelt in the front pew and began to pray.

When Danny finally exited the confessional and came to kneel next to me, I smiled and put my arm around him.

"How did it go?" I whispered.

"Fine, but I was kind of surprised," he replied. "I didn't know there would be a priest in there."

It took me a minute to realize what had happened. In preparing Danny for this day, we had emphasized, over and over again, that it was Jesus he would be meeting in confession. I know we mentioned the priest, but that somehow was not the point that stuck in his young mind. Only the idea of meeting Jesus in the confessional had.

As awkward as I'm sure the realization was for him, I can't really regret that we emphasized Jesus. I need the reminder myself.

There is so much that is awkward about going to confession, and we can get so lost in the distraction of the presence of the priest, our list of sins, the shakiness of our voice, or the words of our prayers, that we miss the point: Jesus is there. It's Jesus who forgives our sins. It's Jesus who touches us in confession.

I once went to confession at a large reconciliation service at the start of Lent. I don't usually receive the sacrament face-to-face, but that was the only option here. There were multiple confession stations set up around the church, and the one I happened to line up at was two kneelers set up face-to-face. The priest knelt in one of them, and we in the line each took our turn kneeling in the other to confess our sins.

It was a little awkward, but I took the occasion to remind myself of the lesson I learned from Danny years ago: It's Jesus we meet in confession. The priest is present, but he is not the one we are there to meet.

At the end of that confession, when the priest said the words of absolution, he placed his hands on my head. This was new territory for a behind-the-screen kind of girl, but I was surprised to find that I didn't feel uncomfortable at all. Through the priest's touch that day, I truly felt the words of absolution as he spoke them:

"God, the Father of mercies, through the death and resurrection of his Son has reconciled the world to himself and sent the Holy Spirit among

us for the forgiveness of sins; through the ministry of the Church may God give you pardon and peace, and I absolve you from your sins in the name of the Father, and of the Son, and of the Holy Spirit."

I absolve you from your sins, Jesus says to us. Just like that, we are forgiven. We are made new. Only God can do that. A priest and his touch reminded me of that truth.

Do you remember the woman that Jesus touched and healed on the Sabbath?

"Now he was teaching in one of the synagogues on the sabbath. And there was a woman who had had a spirit of infirmity for eighteen years; she was bent over and could not fully straighten herself. And when Jesus saw her, he called her and said to her, 'Woman, you are freed from your infirmity.' And he laid his hands upon her, and immediately she was made straight, and she praised God" (Luke 13:10-13).

I used to read stories of miraculous healings like this one and feel that they were very far away. These were exceptional happenings, far from my everyday experiences. In many ways, of course, they are. But, spiritually speaking, every one of us is bent over and cannot fully straighten. Every one of us needs Jesus to touch us, to lay his hands on us, through the sacrament of confession.

Without the heavens opening up and a dove appearing in the sky to announce it, it can be easy to forget that Jesus is truly present to us in the sacraments. As much as I would love a dramatic miracle or sign of God's presence, I think the "everyday" quality of the sacraments can be a gift to us as well.

My parents didn't make a very big deal out of my first confession. They taught me what the sacrament was and how to receive it, and then one week, I got in line with my brothers and sisters and took my turn in there. On the way home, my dad stopped at a convenience store and bought me a candy bar, a taste of the sweetness of forgiveness and a small celebration of the milestone.

In a way, not making a fuss of it was a great gift to me. This is just something we do, their casual approach told me. We all do it. Like taking a shower or eating breakfast or combing our hair, we go to confession. Because it's good for us.

On many Saturday afternoons, after my brothers and sisters and I went to confession, we would run out of the church and stop at a sewer grate in the parking lot. We tore our lists of sins into tiny pieces and threw the bits of paper into the drain.

Often, I was so deeply ashamed of my sins that I would write them in miniature scrawl on the paper. Other times, I could not bring myself to write out my actual sins but would write only a few initials of the words to remind myself of what to say.

I would watch as those tiny pieces of white paper fluttered down the sewer drain, into the darkness below, and feel sweet relief. Here was a tangible sense that my sins were gone, headed back to hell where they belonged. No more secrets.

One of the biggest lies the devil tells us is that we are alone. That we are the only one who ever sins quite like *that*, and it is deeply shameful. So shameful we could never speak such things out loud.

And yet that is precisely the prescription Jesus gives us in the sacrament of confession. Speak the truth out loud. Say your sins. The truth robs sin of its power. Sunlight sanitizes. *You're only as sick as your secrets.* This common saying from many twelve-step programs is a powerful truth. When we speak out loud our secrets, we find freedom and healing in the truth.

God doesn't need us to tell him our sins. He was there. He knows all about it. We are the ones who benefit when we confess our sins. We speak out loud the truth. We show God our wounds and allow him to touch us where we hurt, where we have hurt ourselves, and then we can begin to heal.

This can be hard to do.

My husband Dan and I once spent the weekend at an upscale hotel in Boston. On Sunday morning, as we prepared to leave, the valet pulled our car up to the hotel front doors, and the doorman opened the passenger door for me. And guess what fell out of my car onto the street?

A bunch of garbage. Drive-through wrappers and a discarded glass bottle.

"I'll take care of that for you," the doorman said, stooping to pick up the trash, but I rushed to pick it up myself.

"Oh no," I told him, putting myself between him and the pile of my shame that lay on the street. "You are not touching my garbage!"

We don't like for others to see our garbage. And yet imagine if you had a festering wound on your arm, but when the doctor came into the examination room, you hid it from him because you thought it was too gross for him to see.

We wouldn't do that. We know that we need to show our wounds to the doctor in order to be healed. Sometimes we even need X-rays, MRIs, or other tests to lay bare the truth about what is wrong with us.

We forget that Jesus is a doctor too.

"And as he sat at table in his house, many tax collectors and sinners were sitting with Jesus and his disciples; for there were many who followed him. And the scribes of the Pharisees, when they saw that he was eating with sinners and tax collectors, said to his disciples, 'Why does he eat with tax collectors and sinners?' And when Jesus heard it, he said to them, 'Those who are well have no need of a physician, but those who are sick; I came not to call the righteous but sinners'" (Mark 2:15-17).

We are sick. We are all sick with sin, and Jesus is the physician we need.

I sometimes feel like I can't bring my sickness to Jesus, though. I don't want to stand before him all messy and falling apart. I would rather figure things out for myself and put myself together a bit before approaching God, nice and clean.

But Jesus tells us to come to him, and he heals us exactly as we are, messy and broken, wounded, sick, and fearful. Remember the woman caught in adultery whom the Pharisees threw at the feet of Jesus in order to test him?

They challenged him: *"Teacher, this woman has been caught in the act of adultery. Now in the law Moses commanded us to stone such. What do you say about her?"* (John 8:4-5).

Think of that woman the Pharisees grabbed and threw toward Jesus. Her guilt and shame were fully exposed. If she was "caught in the act of adultery," she probably wasn't even wearing very much clothing. She was vulnerable and exposed.

And isn't this just where we find ourselves sometimes? Thrown at the feet of Jesus, overwhelmed with the shame of our own sinfulness? We think we are alone, but we are not. As he did with the woman caught in adultery, Jesus invites us to look up and see that he is with us.

Jesus did not lie to the woman about the sin she had committed. He gave her the gift of matter-of-fact honesty about her sin, but he did not allow sin to define who she was.

"Neither do I condemn you; go, and do not sin again," he told her (John 8:11).

Likewise, Jesus does not lie to us about what is good and what is evil. He invites us to see the truth, to speak the truth, and thus be touched and healed.

Unlike Jesus, though, our world does lie to us. I sometimes hear people joke about "Catholic guilt," the specific kind of guilt that comes when we do something our faith tells us is wrong but that our culture tells us is perfectly OK. Or at least everyone is doing it and it's no big deal. Taking cultural cues, we can begin to think that everyone lies or everyone cheats or everyone looks at porn or everyone loses their temper.

But sin hurts us, whether we want to recognize the hurt or not. I'll never forget second grade, the year when my best friend's parents were getting a divorce.

"The worst part," she whispered to me one day at school, "is that everyone keeps telling me it's not a big deal."

Our sense of right and wrong is built in. Whether we call it "Catholic guilt" or simply our conscience, we know when we are doing right and when we are doing wrong. It is a big deal. It hurts, and pretending something is OK when it's not only makes it hurt more.

But we need to recognize our capacity to do bad things without falling prey to the equally poisonous lie that we *are* bad. I once heard popular author and speaker Brené Brown give a TED talk in which she described the difference between guilt and shame:

"Shame is a focus on self, guilt is a focus on behavior. Shame is 'I am bad.' Guilt is 'I did something bad.' How many of you, if you did something that was hurtful to me, would be willing to say, 'I'm sorry. I made a mistake?' How many of you would be willing to say that? Guilt: I'm sorry. I made a mistake. Shame: I'm sorry. I am a mistake." [10]

There are two very different perspectives described here. It is God himself who will tell us when we do something bad, and sometimes it is very important that we hear that, but God never tells us that we are bad. He tells us we are made in his image, and that we are good. Very good, in fact.

"God saw everything that he had made, and behold, it was very good" (Genesis 1:31).

God made me very good. Even when I mess up, I can return to him, ask forgiveness, and be made new. I thought of this the other day when I went to confession and found myself, once again, repeating familiar lines to the priest from behind the screen. I had messed up the same stuff. Again. But in the words of absolution, I heard the same reminder that I was forgiven. Again. This is the everyday stuff that real grace is made of. Not the messing up, but the returning to God when we do.

I saw a sign once in a church bathroom: "Wash your hands! Jesus and germs are everywhere." It would be nice if we could just wash our hands once and be clean for good, but the world is a messy place. Sin abounds, but grace abounds too.

When he suffered and died on the Cross, Jesus suffered and died not just for a generic throng of "humanity," but for me. For you. Jesus knew my name and your name, my face and your face, and my sins and your sins when he spoke those words in the last moments before he died: "It is finished."

"He said, 'It is finished'; and he bowed his head and gave up his spirit" (John 19:30).

It is finished. I thought of these words too as I knelt in the quiet church after confession that recent day. We have familiar sins and familiar forgiveness, but we should not become discouraged or dismayed, because we have God's promise. It is finished. We cannot hold onto our sins, because Jesus, the Good Shepherd, has sought us out where we were lost, and he has suffered and died to take our sins away. All that is left is grace.

Give me your grace, Lord. Give me courage to face the things
I have done wrong and the things I continue to do that are wrong.
Help me to see what evils I am attached to and what lies I believe.
Root out my bad habits and open my eyes to the truth about
who I am. Help me to know not only that I am a sinner,
but also that I have been redeemed. Amen.

CHAPTER NINE

God Within Us: Everyday Eucharist

During the first springtime of the COVID-19 pandemic, I grew weary of the word "unprecedented." On a daily basis, the media informed us that these were "unprecedented" times we were living through, our health-care system and economy were undergoing "unprecedented" stresses, our schools and workplaces were being redesigned, and events were being cancelled in "unprecedented" ways.

And pretty much every Catholic I know went weeks without receiving the Eucharist. It was twenty-one weeks for me. Unprecedented.

During the time that many of us were deprived of the sacraments in unprecedented ways, I heard a homily (online, of course) where the priest suggested that this unprecedented time was an opportunity to reflect on what the Eucharist means to us. What the Eucharist is.

Because the Eucharist ... is God. God on earth. God in our hands. God in our mouths. God inside our bodies. We eat him. When our senses tell us otherwise, when our world tells us otherwise, can we possibly believe this unbelievable thing?

I remember being embarrassed many years ago when a Baptist friend of mine in high school questioned me about the Eucharist.

"But you know it's just bread, right?" she said.

"No," I had insisted somewhat sheepishly. "It's Jesus."

"The Eucharist is 'the source and summit of the Christian life,'" we read in the *Catechism*. "The other sacraments, and indeed all ecclesiastical ministries and works of the apostolate, are bound up with the Eucharist and are oriented toward it. For in the blessed Eucharist is contained the whole spiritual good of the Church, namely Christ himself, our Pasch" (*Catechism of the Catholic Church* 1324).

We can use fancy words to describe it, but in the end, that's what the Eucharist is. Jesus.

I like to think of the Eucharist as the *Catechism* describes it, the "source and summit of the Christian life." It's where we come from, it's where we're going, and it's what sustains us along the way.

During that time of pandemic, our pastor, like many good priests, was scrambling to find a way to meet the spiritual needs of his flock without endangering anyone's health. On Palm Sunday, there would be no distribution of palms, but he invited all of us to a parking lot prayer service. We could bring our own "palms" in the form of any branch we found outside, and have our branches blessed, from a safe distance, inside of our cars in the church parking lot.

I walked outside that April morning and found a lush, green hemlock branch. This year, it would be needles instead of palms. I tied a silk ribbon around the branch and figured it looked like a festive blend of Easter and Christmas. New England–style "palms." Some of the kids and I got into the car and drove to the church.

Shall I say it? The prayer service was an unprecedented experience. We pulled into the parking lot and noticed friends we had not seen in weeks pulled in beside us. We waved like maniacs through closed windows and then tuned our radios to the proper station to hear Father, who was standing at the front of all the cars, raising his arms to lead us in prayer.

We prayed a Divine Mercy Chaplet, and then Father disappeared from view and a shuffling noise came over the radio. Eventually, Father reappeared with a host displayed inside a large monstrance and, through the speakers, we heard him sing familiar words of the Eucharistic hymn:

"O salutaris Hostia, / Quae caeli pandis ostium ..."

"O saving Victim, opening wide / The gate of heav'n to man below ..."

Next, Father walked through the parking lot with the monstrance, pausing at each car to offer a benediction with the Blessed Sacrament. We stayed inside our cars and watched as Father approached with the monstrance. When he paused beside our car, I looked at the tiny white host inside that shining gold monstrance, and I caught my breath. My eyes filled with tears. Here was Jesus. After weeks of not seeing him and not receiving him, after weeks of social isolation and spiritual solitude, here he was. In a chilly parking lot in the middle of a slushy New Hampshire spring. I hadn't previously fully recognized that I was missing Jesus in the Eucharist, but I knew it now, as I gazed at him through closed windows from the front seat of my car. I made the Sign of the Cross, and Father moved on.

In the traditional hymn of benediction, the *Tantum Ergo*, we sing,

"Praestet fides supplementum, / Sensuum defectui ..."

"Faith for all defects supplying / where the feeble senses fail ..."

We can't trust our senses. The host that moved me to tears that day appeared, as my Baptist friend would have told me, like nothing more than a small piece of bread. But my faith and my heart told me otherwise.

St. Thérèse of Lisieux once wrote, *"Jesus is there in the Tabernacle expressly for you—for you alone; He is burning with the desire to enter your heart."*[11]

The Eucharist is personal. I certainly knew that in the parking lot. The Eucharist is Jesus, physically and personally present. Jesus, who wants to connect with me and with you, physically and personally.

The Eucharist doesn't seem like a proper sacrament. In fact, it's a scandal. Civilized people simply don't go around eating other people's flesh and blood. It was even a scandal over two thousand years ago when Jesus first spoke about it to his disciples:

"I am the living bread which came down from heaven; if any one eats of this bread, he will live for ever; and the bread which I shall give for the life of the world is my flesh" (John 6:51).

The people listening did not like this teaching. It was weird. It made no sense.

"The Jews then disputed among themselves, saying, 'How can this man give us his flesh to eat?' ... Many of his disciples, when they heard it, said, 'This is a hard saying; who can listen to it?'" (John 6:52, 60).

Exactly! Who can accept it? How can Jesus do such a thing? And yet he did, and he does. Even when those listening to him teach rejected him and walked away, still he insisted that he wanted us to eat his flesh and drink his blood. With even greater clarity this time.

"So Jesus said to them, 'Truly, truly, I say to you, unless you eat the flesh of the Son of man and drink his blood, you have no life in you; he who eats my flesh and drinks my blood has eternal life, and I will raise him up at the last day. For my flesh is food indeed, and my blood is drink indeed. He who eats my flesh and drinks my blood abides in me, and I in him'" (John 6:53-56).

True food. True drink. As uncomfortable as it might make my Baptist friend in high school, as uncomfortable as it might make us as we try to wrap our minds around the impossible notion that God is truly present in the Eucharist, there is nothing merely symbolic here. Jesus is real, and he is really present in the Eucharist.

Because that's how much he loves us. Jesus loves us so much that he wanted not only to pour out his life for us as he hung, bleeding, on the Cross. He wanted a way to stay with us, to physically stay with us, after he returned to heaven. And so here he is, in a tiny wafer.

Will we see him here?

Years ago, when I was very pregnant with Stephen, our fifth child, I sat in the pew one Sunday at Mass. The summer heat in the small church was suffocating. A trickle of sweat ran down the back of my maternity dress, and I sat gasping for breath instead of kneeling during the Eucharistic prayer. Some of the kids crawled in the pew beside me and scrambled into my lap, pawing at my face with sticky hands and drooling into my hair.

And there in the pew, I had a weak moment where I thought I had quite disappeared. Who was I? Where was I?

A tiny person whom I did not yet know twisted and squirmed, kicked and stretched inside my body, taking up my space, using up my energy and my oxygen. My arms and my legs, my face and my hair were overtaken with the other small people in the pew. I was hungry and tired, and yet still they wanted more. All of them wanted all of me.

And that was when I heard the priest speak those familiar words of the Eucharistic prayer: This is my body, given up for you.

"This is my body, given up for you," Jesus tells us in the Eucharist.

"This is my body, given up for you," Jesus tells us from the Cross.

As I sat panting in the pew that Sunday morning, for the first time I understood those words in a physical and personal way. In those words, Jesus not only gives us the gift of himself, he invites us to do the same. For him. And for the people around us.

This is my body, given up for you, I can pray when I am pregnant and tired. *This is my body, given up for you,* I can pray when I am exhausted, stressed, hungry, bored, cold, frustrated, sick, or in pain. *This is my body, given up for you,* I can pray when I make lunches, get up in the middle of the night to change somebody's sheets, when I wipe down the dining room table, vacuum the living room, load the dishwasher, make someone coffee, or stay up late filling out FAFSA forms for college.

There is no crucifixion here, and yet in the Eucharist I hear an invitation to unite my everyday things to Jesus' unfathomable sacrifice on the altar and on the Cross. In the Eucharist, the everyday becomes divine.

Could there be any more basic human need than food? Could there be any more basic food than bread? And yet here, in this very human act of eating humble "bread," we experience an unthinkable physical and spiritual intimacy with God. "Give us this day our daily bread," Jesus teaches us to pray in the Our Father. In the Eucharist, Jesus is our daily bread.

Years ago, my husband and I attended a funeral Mass for a four-month-old baby girl. She was the beloved daughter of Dan's cousin and his wife.

The day after I learned of this tragic loss, I stooped to tie my then three-year-old son's shoelaces.

"Where is God?" he asked me suddenly.

Where, indeed? I wanted to clutch him close and cry. You tell me! Where is God in this mess of a fallen world where sinless babies die and leave their families grieving?

But I didn't do that.

"God is everywhere," I answered, forcing a smile to convince him.

"Yes." He nodded his head knowingly, as if he had been only testing me anyway. "But most of all, he's in the tabba-nacka at church."

Seeing his small mouth work its way around a mispronunciation of "tabernacle," I felt a rush of confidence in his childlike faith. Jesus tells us to have faith like little children; the older and more "grown-up" I get, the more that makes sense to me.

I do believe. But that doesn't mean I don't sometimes falter. I sometimes feel like the anxious father we meet in the Gospel of Mark, the one whose son is possessed by an evil spirit. This is the man to whom Jesus said, "O faithless generation, how long am I to be with you? How long am I to bear with you?" (Mark 9:19).

I am part of that generation. The father's answer to Jesus' question becomes my own humble prayer when I find it hard to have faith.

"I believe," the man told Jesus shakily. "Help my unbelief" (Mark 9:24).

Help our unbelief. We have to believe. In the face of grief, sorrow, loss, and pain in this world, the only alternative is to become jaded and indifferent.

"The most deadly poison of our times is indifference ..." St. Maximilian Kolbe once said. "And this happens, although the praise of God should know no limits. ... Let us strive therefore to praise Him to the greatest extent of our powers."[12]

Our world certainly has its share of indifference. We can walk past a huddled mass of homeless people on a city street as if they were part of the landscape, not seeing their humanity. We can fire off an angry reply in response to someone's political opinion on social media, forgetting the person and the story behind their words. We can give way to frustration and dismiss entire segments of the world population as lazy or violent or stupid or worthless.

Sacrificing ourselves for the sake of another makes no sense in the modern world, where we are encouraged to look out for ourselves and seek our own wealth, status, and pleasure, often at the cost of our fellow human beings. But the antidote to indifference is the total self-giving love that Jesus gives to us in the Eucharist. *This is my body, given up for you.* We need to practice that kind of giving, and in the Eucharist, Jesus gives us strength to do it.

From the moment he was born, Jesus was already foreshadowing the gift that he had come to earth to give. In place of a crib, baby Jesus slept in a manger. A manger is a trough, a structure used to hold food for animals. The very word "manger" comes from the French word *manger*—to eat. Baby Jesus, asleep on the hay, was already telling us, "This is my body, given up for you." He was already feeding us.

On some days, I am tempted to think the idea of the Eucharist and the ways I am called to live it out in the everyday are ludicrous. One recent Tuesday morning, I woke up early to focus on some writing work I needed to get done. I sat alone in the dining room and worked for three hours before anyone else in my house was awake. When they did get up, one child needed me to make a phone call to change a dental appointment, another one wanted a ride to a friend's house, and a third one asked me to help him write a letter for an internship he was applying for. Legitimate needs, every one of them, and I did what they asked.

A phone conference call and a Zoom meeting later, I had a list of work responsibilities for the rest of my day that would take me straight into the evening hours. Then I got an email explaining that the videos I had recorded for promoting an upcoming retreat weren't quite what the church needed. Could I record them again, vertically this time? Real quick?

I still needed to make a plan for dinner, unload the dishwasher, drive one kid to her part-time job, and pick up a prescription at the pharmacy. When a friend texted in the midst of it all, asking if I could meet for coffee that afternoon because she really wanted to talk to me about a problem she was having with her sister, I felt my blood pressure rise.

I was tired. Everybody wanted a piece of me, and I felt thoroughly consumed. How on earth did all the people in my life become so needy?

The fact is, we are all needy. And no one was trying to nail me to a cross that particular afternoon, so perhaps my complaint was invalid. But this is a familiar struggle. I want to say the words and mean them: *This is my body, given up for you. This is me. I am ... for you.* And yet it's so hard sometimes to live that out and not feel like I'm floundering beneath the weight of it all.

When I struggle to "feed" my people, I like to think about another Gospel story where Jesus fed his disciples. Remember the fish breakfast they had together on the beach?

"When they got out on land, they saw a charcoal fire there, with fish lying on it, and bread. Jesus said to them, 'Bring some of the fish that you have just caught.' So Simon Peter went aboard and hauled the net ashore, full of large fish, a hundred and fifty-three of them; and although there were so many, the net was not torn. Jesus said to them, 'Come and have breakfast'" (John 21:9-12).

Come and have breakfast. What a delightful invitation! I want to have grilled fish and bread on the beach with Jesus! When we are weary from feeding the masses, from fishing all night, Jesus invites us to sit down with him and have something to eat.

One small detail of this story that always stands out to me is the part about the nets. There were so many fish—153 of them, I wonder who counted?—and yet "although there were so many, the net was not torn."

When God uses me to catch his fish and to feed his people, I sometimes feel like I might tear or I might break. There are just so many people who need so many things. I get tired and impatient; I grow hungry myself. And yet Jesus gives us courage to believe that when we give, and when we continue to give, sometimes past our initial hesitations, and sometimes forgetting our own comforts, we will not tear and we will not break. Don't worry about that, he reassures us as he smiles and waves from shore. Come and eat. This is my body, given up for you.

In that moment we looked at earlier, where Jesus first spoke about the Eucharist in explicit terms and the people who could not accept this uncomfortable teaching walked away, rejecting him, Jesus turned to his remaining disciples with a question.

"After this many of his disciples drew back and no longer walked with him. Jesus said to the Twelve, 'Will you also go away?'" (John 6:66-67).

He turns to me and asks me this too. Are you uncomfortable? Is this too much? Do you also wish to go away?

In all of my discomfort, in all of my everyday moments, I want my response to be the same as Simon Peter's reply in that moment there: *"Lord, to whom shall we go? You have the words of eternal life"* (John 6:68).

This teaching is difficult; who can accept it? I can. I want to. I will.

Feed me, Lord. In all the ways I am empty, fill me up. In all the places I am weak, make me strong. Fix all of my broken places and heal my wounds. Give me your grace, your light, your goodness, and your life. Fill me with every part of you until I overflow with your truth, mercy, and love and can feed your people with it. I want to receive the gift of you fully, now and always. Amen.

CHAPTER TEN

Everyday Places: Beginning to See

When I read the stories of Jesus' life in the Gospels, I'm sometimes amazed by the cluelessness of the people he lived with and spoke to. They were so obtuse. There they were, walking around with Jesus. They were hanging out with God, and yet most of them had no idea who he was.

I like to think I wouldn't miss God's presence in such an obvious way. Take this scene, for example, where Jesus reads the words of Scripture in the Temple for the first time.

"He stood up to read; and there was given to him the book of the prophet Isaiah. He opened the book and found the place where it was written, 'The Spirit of the Lord is upon me, because he has anointed me to preach good news to the poor. He has sent me to proclaim release to the captives and recovering of sight to the blind, to set at liberty those who are oppressed, to proclaim the acceptable year of the Lord.' And he closed the book, and gave it back to the attendant, and sat down; and the eyes of all in the synagogue were fixed on him. And he began to say to them, 'Today this Scripture has been fulfilled in your hearing.' And all spoke well of him, and wondered at the gracious words which proceeded out of his mouth" (Luke 4:16-22).

This is such a mic-drop moment. I can just imagine the heavens opening up and harps playing as Jesus reads the prophetic words of Isaiah. Everyone takes notice. And then, in case they missed it, when Jesus sits back down, he tells everyone plainly, "Today this scripture has been fulfilled in your hearing."

And yet I'm sure most of the people present that day, amazed though they were, missed the entire point. It's not their fault, really. We don't expect Scripture to be fulfilled in our hearing. But it is fulfilled in our hearing every day. Part of what I have tried to do in the pages of this book is remind myself of that.

I want to see God where he sits in the everyday places of everyday life. I want to hear his voice when he speaks to me in the ordinary moments of ordinary living. I don't want to miss what is being fulfilled in my hearing today. I want to experience God where he is: right here, right now.

When I told my husband that I was planning to write a book about being an everyday mystic, he got serious. "If you are going to be a mystic," he said, "you'll need a whole new wardrobe."

It's true. Mystics don't wear jeggings with an oversized sweatshirt they bought in Cape Cod last summer. They wear flowing robes. Holiness emanates from their very being. They glow. They shine. They radiate wisdom.

I'm not that kind of mystic.

But I don't want to be so focused on other people's extraordinary experiences of God that I miss my own ordinary ones. So maybe I can be an everyday mystic. The kind that slows down enough sometimes to see God in other people, in joy, in pain, in contentment, in stillness, in inspiration, and in prayer. Someone who pauses just long enough sometimes to wonder at the power of God's presence in the sacraments. Someone who recognizes everyday places and everyday experiences where we can see God, hear him, feel him, and know him.

I want to do that. If I can do that, even if Jesus never appears at my bedside, even if the clouds never part and a booming voice never tells me that I am his daughter and that he is well pleased, it will be enough.

It will be enough to pull back the curtain a tiny bit sometimes and see where God is, flowing like a mighty river all around us, like a great surge of water roaring over our heads. It's OK if only sometimes I feel myself swept up in that flood.

It will be enough to quiet my heart just enough sometimes to be able to hear the chorus of heaven singing its resounding, endless hymns of praise, echoing all around us. It's OK if only sometimes I feel myself begin to sing.

It will be enough to sit still just long enough sometimes to feel God where he is, in every beat of my heart, in every cell of my body, in my every waking moment, every thought and every dream. It's OK if only sometimes I feel him within my grasp.

It might take the rest of my days for me to learn how to quiet my inner self, but I want to stop seeking and allow myself to be found. I want to stop trying to meet God where he is, and instead I want to be where I am. I want to let God find me here.

And when God finds me, I want to be still. I want to rest in him, the almighty God, a God who is so great that we can spend a lifetime looking and only just begin to see.

Everyday Prayers

For your inspiration, here is a collection of favorite prayers, from Church liturgy and tradition and from the saints. Some of them are mentioned in the chapters of this book, and others are just favorites of mine, old and new.

Act of Faith

O my God, I firmly believe
that you are one God in three divine Persons,
Father, Son, and Holy Spirit.
I believe that your divine Son became man
and died for our sins and that he will come
to judge the living and the dead.
I believe these and all the truths
which the Holy Catholic Church teaches
because you have revealed them
who are eternal truth and wisdom,
who can neither deceive nor be deceived.
In this faith I intend to live and die.
Amen.[13]

Act of Hope

O Lord God,
I hope by your grace for the pardon
of all my sins
and after life here to gain eternal happiness
because you have promised it
who are infinitely powerful, faithful, kind,
and merciful.
In this hope I intend to live and die.
Amen.[14]

Act of Love

O Lord God, I love you above all things
and I love my neighbor for your sake
because you are the highest, infinite and perfect
good, worthy of all my love.
In this love I intend to live and die.
Amen.[15]

The Te Deum

You are God: we praise you;
You are God: we acclaim you;
You are the eternal Father:
All creation worships you.
To you all angels, all the powers of heaven,
Cherubim and Seraphim, sing in endless praise:
Holy, holy, holy, Lord, God of power and might,
Heaven and earth are full of your glory.
The glorious company of apostles praise you.
The noble fellowship of prophets praise you.
The white-robed army of martyrs praise you.
Throughout the world the holy Church acclaims you:
Father, of majesty unbounded,
Your true and only Son, worthy of all worship,
And the Holy Spirit, advocate and guide.
You, Christ, are the king of glory,
The eternal Son of the Father.
When you became man to set us free,
You did not spurn the Virgin's womb.
You overcame the sting of death,
And opened the kingdom of heaven to all believers.
You are seated at God's right hand in glory.
We believe that you will come, and be our judge.
Come then, Lord, and help your people,
Bought with the price of your own blood,

And bring us with your saints
To glory everlasting.
Save your people, Lord, and bless your inheritance.
Govern and uphold them now and always.
Day by day we bless you.
We praise your name forever.
Keep us today, Lord, from all sin.
Have mercy on us, Lord, have mercy.
Lord, show us your love and mercy;
For we put our trust in you.
In you, Lord, is our hope:
And we shall never hope in vain.[16]

Prayer to the Holy Spirit

Breathe in me, O Holy Spirit, that all my thoughts may be holy.
Act in me, O Holy Spirit, that my work, too, may be holy.

Draw my heart, O Holy Spirit, that I may love only what is holy.
Strengthen me, O Holy Spirit, to defend all that is holy.

Guard me, then, O Holy Spirit, that I always may be holy. Amen.

–attributed to St. Augustine

Come, Holy Spirit

Come, Holy Spirit, fill the hearts of thy faithful and enkindle in
them the fire of thy love.

V. Send forth thy spirit and they shall be created.

R. And thou shalt renew the face of the earth.

Let us pray. O God, who didst instruct the hearts of the faithful
by the light of the Holy Spirit, grant us in the same spirit to be
truly wise, and ever to rejoice in his consolation. Through Christ
Our Lord. Amen.

Prayer of Self-Dedication to Christ

Take, Lord, and receive all my liberty,
my memory, my understanding,
and my entire will,
all I have and call my own.
You have given all to me.
To you, Lord, I return it.
Everything is yours; do with it what you will.
Give me only your love and your grace,
that is enough for me.[17]

–St. Ignatius of Loyola

Prayer of Dedication

Lord Jesus,
I give you my hands to do your work.
I give you my feet to follow your way.
I give you my eyes to see as you do.
I give you my tongue to speak your words.
I give you my mind so you can think in me.
I give you my spirit so you can pray in me.
Above all, I give you my heart
So in me you can love your Father and all people.
I give you my whole self so you can grow in me,
Till it is you, Lord Jesus,
Who lives and works and prays in me. Amen.[18]

Prayer for Generosity

Dearest Lord, teach me to be generous. Teach me to serve Thee
as Thou deservest: to give and not to count the cost; to fight and
not to heed the wounds; to toil and not to seek for rest; to labor
and not to seek reward, save that of knowing that I do Thy Will,
O God.[19]

–St. Ignatius of Loyola

Prayer to Seek God

Lord Jesus, let me know myself and know you,
And desire nothing, save only you.
Let me hate myself and love you.
Let me do everything for the sake of you.
Let me humble myself and exalt you.
Let me think of nothing except you.
Let me die to myself and live in you.
Let me accept whatever happens as from you.
Let me banish self and follow you,
And ever desire to follow you.
Let me fly from myself and take refuge in you,
That I may deserve to be defended by you.
Let me fear for myself, let me fear you,
And let me be among those who are chosen by you.
Let me distrust myself and put my trust in you.
Let me be willing to obey for the sake of you.
Let me cling to nothing, save only to you,
And let me be poor because of you.
Look upon me, that I may love you.
Call me, that I may see you,
And for ever enjoy you.
Amen.[20]

–St. Augustine

Anima Christi

Soul of Christ, sanctify me.
Body of Christ, save me.
Blood of Christ, inebriate me.
Water out of the side of Christ, wash me.
Passion of Christ, strengthen me.
O good Jesus, hear me;
Hide me within Thy wounds;
Suffer me not to be separated from Thee;
Defend me from the malignant enemy;

Call me at the hour of my death,
And bid me come unto Thee,
That with Thy saints I may praise Thee
For all eternity. Amen.[21]

Mission Prayer

God has created me to do Him some definite service; He has committed some work to me which He has not committed to another. I have my mission—I never may know it in this life, but I shall be told it in the next. ... I am a link in a chain, a bond of connection between persons. He has not created me for naught. I shall do good, I shall do His work; I shall be an angel of peace, a preacher of truth in my own place, while not intending it, if I do but keep His commandments. ... Therefore I will trust Him. Whatever, wherever I am, I can never be thrown away. If I am in sickness, my sickness may serve Him; in perplexity, my perplexity may serve Him; if I am in sorrow, my sorrow may serve him. ... He does nothing in vain. ... He knows what He is about. He may take away my friends, He may throw me among strangers, He may make me feel desolate, make my spirits sink, hide the future from me—still He knows what He is about.[22]

–St. John Henry Newman

Presence of Jesus Prayer

Dear Jesus, help me to spread Thy fragrance everywhere I go. Flood my soul with Thy spirit and love. Penetrate and possess my whole being so utterly that all my life may only be a radiance of Thine. Shine through me and be so in me that every soul I come in contact with may feel Thy presence in my soul. Let them look up and see no longer me but only Jesus. Stay with me and then I shall begin to shine as you shine, so to shine as to be a light to others. Amen.[23]

Prayer of Peace

Lord, make me an instrument of your peace:
where there is hatred, let me sow love;
where there is injury, pardon;
where there is doubt, faith;
where there is despair, hope;
where there is darkness, light;
where there is sadness, joy.
O divine Master, grant that I may not so much seek
to be consoled as to console,
to be understood as to understand,
to be loved as to love.
For it is in giving that we receive,
it is in pardoning that we are pardoned,
and it is in dying that we are born to eternal life.
Amen.[24]

–St. Francis of Assisi

Bookmark of St. Teresa of Avila

Let nothing disturb you. Let nothing frighten you. All things pass
away. God never changes. Patience obtains all things. They who
have God lack nothing. God alone is enough.[25]

–St. Teresa of Avila

Mission Prayer

Christ has no body now on earth but yours, no hands but yours,
no feet but yours; yours are the eyes through which he looks
compassion on this world; yours are the feet with which he is to
go about doing good. Amen.

–Anonymous

Prayer for Good Humor

Grant me, O Lord, good digestion, and also something to digest.
Grant me a healthy body, and the necessary good humor to
maintain it.
Grant me a simple soul that knows to treasure all that is good
and that doesn't frighten easily at the sight of evil,
but rather finds the means to put things back in their place.
Give me a soul that knows not boredom, grumbling, sighs and
laments,
nor excess of stress, because of that obstructing thing called "I".
Grant me, O Lord, a sense of good humor.
Allow me the grace to be able to take a joke and to discover in
life a bit of joy,
and to be able to share it with others.[26]

Prayer for Strength

God, our Father, we are exceedingly frail and indisposed to every
virtuous and gallant undertaking. Strengthen our weakness,
we beseech you, that we may do valiantly in this spiritual war;
help us against our own negligence and cowardice, and defend
us from the treachery of our unfaithful hearts, for Jesus Christ's
sake. Amen.[27]

–Thomas à Kempis

Daily Offering

Into your hands, O Lord, and into the hands of your holy
angels, I commit and entrust this day my soul, my relations, my
benefactors, my friends and enemies, and all your ... people.
Keep us, O Lord, through the day, by the merits and intercession
of the Blessed Virgin Mary and of all your saints, from all vicious
and unruly desires, from all sins and temptations of the devil,
and from sudden and unprovided death and the pains of hell.
Illuminate my heart with the grace of your Holy Spirit; grant that

I may ever be obedient to your commandments; suffer me not to be separated from you, O God. Amen.[28]

–St. Edmund

Prayer to Do God's Will

Grant me, O merciful God, that what is pleasing to you I may ardently desire, prudently acquire, truthfully acknowledge, and perfectly accomplish for the praise and glory of your name. Amen.[29]

–St. Thomas Aquinas

Daily Prayer

... I arise today
Through the strength of heaven;
Light of the sun,
Splendor of fire,
Speed of lightning,
Swiftness of the wind,
Depth of the sea,
Stability of the earth,
Firmness of the rock.
I arise today
Through God's strength to pilot me;
God's might to uphold me,
God's wisdom to guide me,
God's eye to look before me,
God's ear to hear me,
God's word to speak for me,
God's hand to guard me,
God's way to lie before me,
God's shield to protect me,
God's hosts to save me ...
Afar and anear,
Alone or in a multitude ...
Christ shield me today ...

Against wounding ...
Christ with me, Christ before me, Christ behind me,
Christ in me, Christ beneath me, Christ above me,
Christ on my right, Christ on my left,
Christ when I lie down, Christ when I sit down,
Christ in the heart of every man who thinks of me,
Christ in the mouth of every man who speaks of me,
Christ in the eye that sees me,
Christ in the ear that hears me.
I arise today
Through a mighty strength, the invocation of the Trinity ...
Amen.[30]

–St. Patrick

Prayer for Seekers of Faith

Gracious and holy Father,
give us the wisdom to discover you,
the intelligence to understand you,
the diligence to seek after you,
the patience to wait for you,
eyes to behold you,
a heart to meditate on you,
and a life to proclaim you,
through the power of the Spirit of Jesus, our Lord.[31]

Prayer to Seek God

O Lord, my God,
teach my heart this day where and how to see you,
where and how to find you.
You have made me and remade me,
and you have bestowed on me
all the good things I possess,
and still I do not know you.
I have not yet done that
for which I was made.

Teach me to seek you,
for I cannot seek you
unless you teach me,
or find you
unless you show yourself to me.
Let me seek you in my desire;
let me desire you in my seeking.
Let me find you by loving you;
let me love you when I find you.[32]

Morning Offering

O Jesus,
through the Immaculate Heart of Mary,
I offer you my prayers, works, joys and sufferings of this day
for all the intentions of your Sacred Heart,
in union with the Holy Sacrifice of the Mass throughout the
world,
in reparation for my sins,
for the intentions of all my relatives and friends,
and in particular for the intentions of the Holy Father.
Amen.

Bedtime Prayer

Watch, O Lord, with those who wake,
or watch, or weep tonight,
and give your angels charge over those who sleep.
Tend your sick ones, O Lord Christ.
Rest your weary ones.
Bless your dying ones.
Soothe your suffering ones.
Pity your afflicted ones.
Shield your joyous ones.
And for all your love's sake.
Amen.[33]

Prayer to St. Michael the Archangel

St. Michael the Archangel, defend us in battle. Be our protection against the wickedness and snares of the devil. May God rebuke him, we humbly pray, and do thou, O Prince of the Heavenly Host, by the power of God, cast into hell Satan and all the evil spirits, who prowl throughout the world seeking the ruin of souls. Amen.

The Litany of Humility

O Jesus, meek and humble of heart,
Make my heart like yours.
From self-will, deliver me, O Lord.
From the desire of being esteemed, deliver me, O Lord.
From the desire of being loved, deliver me, O Lord.
From the desire of being extolled, deliver me, O Lord.
From the desire of being honored, deliver me, O Lord.
From the desire of being praised, deliver me, O Lord.
From the desire of being preferred to others, deliver me, O Lord.
From the desire of being consulted, deliver me, O Lord.
From the desire of being approved, deliver me, O Lord.
From the desire to be understood, deliver me, O Lord.
From the desire to be visited, deliver me, O Lord.
From the fear of being humiliated, deliver me, O Lord.
From the fear of being despised, deliver me, O Lord.
From the fear of suffering rebukes, deliver me, O Lord.
From the fear of being calumniated, deliver me, O Lord.
From the fear of being forgotten, deliver me, O Lord.
From the fear of being ridiculed, deliver me, O Lord.
From the fear of being suspected, deliver me, O Lord.
From the fear of being wronged, deliver me, O Lord.
From the fear of being abandoned, deliver me, O Lord.
From the fear of being refused, deliver me, O Lord.
That others may be loved more than I,
Lord, grant me the grace to desire it.
That, in the opinion of the world, others may increase

and I may decrease,
Lord, grant me the grace to desire it.
That others may be chosen and I set aside,
Lord, grant me the grace to desire it.
That others may be praised and I go unnoticed,
Lord, grant me the grace to desire it.
That others may be preferred to me in everything,
Lord, grant me the grace to desire it.
That others may become holier than I, provided that I may
become as holy as I should,
Lord, grant me the grace to desire it. ...
Amen.[34]

Litany of Trust

by Sr. Faustina Maria Pia, SV

From the belief that I have to earn Your love
　　Deliver me, Jesus.
From the fear that I am unlovable
　　Deliver me, Jesus.
From the false security that I have what it takes
　　Deliver me, Jesus.
From the fear that trusting You will leave me more destitute
　　Deliver me, Jesus.
From all suspicion of Your words and promises
　　Deliver me, Jesus.
From the rebellion against childlike dependency on You
　　Deliver me, Jesus.
From refusals and reluctances in accepting Your will
　　Deliver me, Jesus.
From anxiety about the future
　　Deliver me, Jesus.
From resentment or excessive preoccupation with the past
　　Deliver me, Jesus.
From restless self-seeking in the present moment
　　Deliver me, Jesus.

From disbelief in Your love and presence
　　Deliver me, Jesus.
From the fear of being asked to give more than I have
　　Deliver me, Jesus.
From the belief that my life has no meaning or worth
　　Deliver me, Jesus.
From the fear of what love demands
　　Deliver me, Jesus.
From discouragement
　　Deliver me, Jesus.

That You are continually holding me, sustaining me, loving me
　　Jesus, I trust in You.
That Your love goes deeper than my sins and failings, and transforms me
　　Jesus, I trust in You.
That not knowing what tomorrow brings is an invitation to lean on You
　　Jesus, I trust in You.
That You are with me in my suffering
　　Jesus, I trust in You.
That my suffering, united to Your own, will bear fruit in this life and the next
　　Jesus, I trust in You.
That You will not leave me orphan, that You are present in Your Church
　　Jesus, I trust in You.
That Your plan is better than anything else
　　Jesus, I trust in You.
That You always hear me and in Your goodness always respond to me
　　Jesus, I trust in You.
That You give me the grace to accept forgiveness and to forgive others
　　Jesus, I trust in You.
That You give me all the strength I need for what is asked
　　Jesus, I trust in You.

That my life is a gift
  Jesus, I trust in You.
That You will teach me to trust You
  Jesus, I trust in You.
That You are my Lord and my God
  Jesus, I trust in You.
That I am Your beloved one
  Jesus, I trust in You.[35]

Everyday Scripture

Following are quotations from Scripture that I hope will inspire further meditation on the themes of each of the chapters in this book. If you don't know how to pray or where to begin, begin here. Read one small passage slowly and carefully. Read it again and see if a word or a phrase stands out to you. Then hold that phrase in your mind, repeat it, and ask God for the grace of hearing his voice in it. God is present. God is faithful. You will see.

CHAPTER ONE

Breaking Boundaries: Encountering God in Other People

"Then the King will say to those at his right hand, 'Come, O blessed of my Father, inherit the kingdom prepared for you from the foundation of the world; for I was hungry and you gave me food, I was thirsty and you gave me drink, I was a stranger and you welcomed me, I was naked and you clothed me, I was sick and you visited me, I was in prison and you came to me.' Then the righteous will answer him, 'Lord, when did we see you hungry and feed you, or thirsty and give you drink? And when did we see you a stranger and welcome you, or naked and clothe you? And when did we see you sick or in prison and visit you?' And the King will answer them, 'Truly, I say to you, as you did it to one of the least of these my brethren, you did it to me.'"

–Matthew 25:34-40

"But I say to you that hear, Love your enemies, do good to those who hate you, bless those who curse you, pray for those who abuse you. To him who strikes you on the cheek, offer the other also; and from him who takes away your cloak do not withhold your coat as well. Give to every one who begs from you; and of him who takes away your goods do not ask them again. And as you wish that men would do to you, do so to them.

"If you love those who love you, what credit is that to you? For even sinners love those who love them. And if you do good to those who do good to you, what credit is that to you? For even sinners do the same. And if you lend to those from whom you hope to receive, what credit is that to you? Even sinners lend to sinners, to receive as much again. But love your enemies, and do good, and lend, expecting nothing in return; and your reward will be great, and you will be sons of the Most High; for he is kind to the ungrateful and the selfish. Be merciful, even as your Father is merciful."

–Luke 6:27-36

The point is this: he who sows sparingly will also reap sparingly, and he who sows bountifully will also reap bountifully. Each one must do as he has made up his mind, not reluctantly or under compulsion, for God loves a cheerful giver. And God is able to provide you with every blessing in abundance, so that you may always have enough of everything and may provide in abundance for every good work.

–2 Corinthians 9:6-8

We know that we have passed out of death into life, because we love the brethren. He who does not love remains in death. Any one who hates his brother is a murderer, and you know that no murderer has eternal life abiding in him. By this we know love, that he laid down his life for us; and we ought to lay down our lives for the brethren. But if any one has the world's goods and sees his brother in need, yet closes his heart against him, how does God's love abide in him? Little children, let us not love in word or speech but in deed and in truth.

–1 John 3:14-18

CHAPTER TWO

Tasting Goodness: Finding God in Joy

And God blessed them, and God said to them, "Be fruitful and multiply, and fill the earth and subdue it; and have dominion over the fish of the sea and over the birds of the air and over every living thing that moves upon the earth." And God said, "Behold, I have given you every plant yielding seed which is upon the face of all the earth, and every tree with seed in its fruit; you shall have them for food. And to every beast of the earth, and to every bird of the air, and to everything that creeps on the earth, everything that has the breath of life, I have given every green plant for food." And it was so. And God saw everything that he had made, and behold, it was very good.

–Genesis 1:28-31

I will greatly rejoice in the LORD,
my soul shall exult in my God;
for he has clothed me with the garments of salvation,
he has covered me with the robe of righteousness,
as a bridegroom decks himself with a garland,
and as a bride adorns herself with her jewels.
For as the earth brings forth its shoots,
and as a garden causes what is sown in it to spring up,
so the Lord GOD will cause righteousness and praise
to spring forth before all the nations.

–Isaiah 61:10-11

The stone which the builders rejected
has become the cornerstone.
This is the LORD's doing;
it is marvelous in our eyes.
This is the day which the LORD has made;
let us rejoice and be glad in it.

–Psalm 118:22-24

I bless the LORD who gives me counsel;
in the night also my heart instructs me.
I keep the LORD always before me;
because he is at my right hand, I shall not be moved.

Therefore my heart is glad, and my soul rejoices;
my body also dwells secure.
For you do not give me up to Sheol,
or let your godly one see the Pit.

You show me the path of life;
in your presence there is fulness of joy,
in your right hand are pleasures for evermore.

–Psalm 16:7-11

CHAPTER THREE

Leaning In: Seeing God in Pain

Yet it was the will of the LORD to bruise him;
he has put him to grief;

when he makes himself an offering for sin,
he shall see his offspring, he shall prolong his days;

the will of the LORD shall prosper in his hand;
he shall see the fruit of the travail of his soul and be
satisfied;

by his knowledge shall the righteous one, my servant,
make many to be accounted righteous;
and he shall bear their iniquities.

–Isaiah 53:10-11

Jesus answered them, "Do you now believe? The hour is
coming, indeed it has come, when you will be scattered,
every man to his home, and will leave me alone; yet I am
not alone, for the Father is with me. I have said this to
you, that in me you may have peace. In the world you
have tribulation; but be of good cheer, I have overcome
the world."

–John 16:31-33

Then he said to them, "My soul is very sorrowful, even
to death; remain here, and watch with me." And going a
little farther he fell on his face and prayed, "My Father, if
it be possible, let this chalice pass from me; nevertheless,
not as I will, but as you will."

–Matthew 26:38-39

We know that in everything God works for good with those who love him, who are called according to his purpose.

–Romans 8:28

No, in all these things we are more than conquerors through him who loved us. For I am sure that neither death, nor life, nor angels, nor principalities, nor things present, nor things to come, nor powers, nor height, nor depth, nor anything else in all creation, will be able to separate us from the love of God in Christ Jesus our Lord.

–Romans 8:37-39

"Truly, truly, I say to you, you will weep and lament, but the world will rejoice; you will be sorrowful, but your sorrow will turn into joy. When a woman is in labor, she has pain, because her hour has come; but when she is delivered of the child, she no longer remembers the anguish, for joy that a child is born into the world. So you have sorrow now, but I will see you again and your hearts will rejoice, and no one will take your joy from you. In that day you will ask nothing of me. Truly, truly, I say to you, if you ask anything of the Father, he will give it to you in my name. Until now you have asked nothing in my name; ask, and you will receive, that your joy may be full."

–John 16:20-24

CHAPTER FOUR

Letting Go: Discovering God in Contentment

"And when you pray, you must not be like the hypocrites; for they love to stand and pray in the synagogues and at the street corners, that they may be seen by men. Truly, I say to you, they have their reward. But when you pray, go into your room and shut the door and pray to your Father who is in secret; and your Father who sees in secret will reward you."

–Matthew 6:5-6

"And when you fast, do not look dismal, like the hypocrites, for they disfigure their faces that their fasting may be seen by men. Truly, I say to you, they have their reward. But when you fast, anoint your head and wash your face, that your fasting may not be seen by men but by your Father who is in secret; and your Father who sees in secret will reward you."

–Matthew 6:16-18

"But if God so clothes the grass of the field, which today is alive and tomorrow is thrown into the oven, will he not much more clothe you, O you of little faith? Therefore do not be anxious, saying, 'What shall we eat?' or 'What shall we drink?' or 'What shall we wear?' For the Gentiles seek all these things; and your heavenly Father knows that you need them all. But seek first his kingdom and his righteousness, and all these things shall be yours as well."

–Matthew 6:30-33

I rejoice in the Lord greatly that now at length you have revived your concern for me; you were indeed concerned for me, but you had no opportunity. Not that I complain of want; for I have learned, in whatever state I am, to be content. I know how to be abased, and I know how to abound; in any and all circumstances I have learned the secret of facing plenty and hunger, abundance and want. I can do all things in him who strengthens me.

–Philippians 4:10-13

CHAPTER FIVE

Slowing Down: Seeking God in Stillness

And taking the five loaves and the two fish he looked up to heaven, and blessed, and broke and gave the loaves to the disciples, and the disciples gave them to the crowds. And they all ate and were satisfied. And they took up twelve baskets full of the broken pieces left over. And those who ate were about five thousand men, besides women and children.

–Matthew 14:19-21

And a great storm of wind arose, and the waves beat into the boat, so that the boat was already filling. But he was in the stern, asleep on the cushion; and they woke him and said to him, "Teacher, do you not care if we perish?" And he awoke and rebuked the wind, and said to the sea, "Peace! Be still!" And the wind ceased, and there was a great calm. He said to them, "Why are you afraid? Have you no faith?"

–Mark 4:37-40

Now as they went on their way, he entered a village; and a woman named Martha received him into her house. And she had a sister called Mary, who sat at the Lord's feet and listened to his teaching. But Martha was distracted with much serving; and she went to him and said, "Lord, do you not care that my sister has left me to serve alone? Tell her then to help me." But the Lord answered her, "Martha, Martha, you are anxious and troubled about many things; one thing is needful. Mary has chosen the good portion, which shall not be taken away from her."

–Luke 10:38-42

"Be still, and know that I am God.
*   I am exalted among the nations,*
*   I am exalted in the earth!"*
The LORD of hosts is with us;
*   the God of Jacob is our refuge.*

–Psalm 46:10-11

And in the morning, a great while before day, he rose and went out to a lonely place, and there he prayed.

–Mark 1:35

And after he had dismissed the crowds, he went up into the hills by himself to pray. When evening came, he was there alone.

–Matthew 14:23

In these days he went out to the hills to pray; and all night he continued in prayer to God.

–Luke 6:12

But so much the more the report went abroad concerning him; and great multitudes gathered to hear and to be healed of their infirmities. But he withdrew to the wilderness and prayed.

–Luke 5:15-16

CHAPTER SIX

Tuning In: Hearing God in Inspiration

And suddenly a sound came from heaven like the rush of a mighty wind, and it filled all the house where they were sitting. And there appeared to them tongues as of fire, distributed and resting on each one of them. And they were all filled with the Holy Spirit and began to speak in other tongues, as the Spirit gave them utterance.

–Acts 2:2-4

"And I will ask the Father, and he will give you another Counselor, to be with you for ever, even the Spirit of truth, whom the world cannot receive, because it neither sees him nor knows him; you know him, for he dwells with you, and will be in you."

–John 14:16-17

More than that, we rejoice in our sufferings, knowing that suffering produces endurance, and endurance produces character, and character produces hope, and hope does not disappoint us, because God's love has been poured into our hearts through the Holy Spirit who has been given to us.

–Romans 5:3-5

"And the gospel must first be preached to all nations. And when they bring you to trial and deliver you up, do not be anxious beforehand about what you are to say; but say whatever is given you in that hour, for it is not you who speak, but the Holy Spirit."

–Mark 13:10-11

"It is the Spirit that gives life, the flesh is of no avail; the words that I have spoken to you are Spirit and life."

–John 6:63

"I have yet many things to say to you, but you cannot bear them now. When the Spirit of truth comes, he will guide you into all the truth; for he will not speak on his own authority, but whatever he hears he will speak, and he will declare to you the things that are to come. He will glorify me, for he will take what is mine and declare it to you. All that the Father has is mine; therefore I said that he will take what is mine and declare it to you."

–John 16:12-15

"Seek the LORD *while he may be found,*
call upon him while he is near;
let the wicked forsake his way,
and the unrighteous man his thoughts;
let him return to the LORD, *that he may have mercy on him,*
and to our God, for he will abundantly pardon.
For my thoughts are not your thoughts,
neither are your ways my ways, says the LORD.
For as the heavens are higher than the earth,
so are my ways higher than your ways
and my thoughts than your thoughts."

–Isaiah 55:6-9

CHAPTER SEVEN

Journeying On: Meeting God in Prayer

Rejoice always, pray constantly, give thanks in all
circumstances; for this is the will of God in Christ Jesus
for you.

–1 Thessalonians 5:16-18

"The Pharisee stood and prayed thus with himself, 'God,
I thank you that I am not like other men, extortioners,
unjust, adulterers, or even like this tax collector. I fast
twice a week, I give tithes of all that I get.' But the tax
collector, standing far off, would not even lift up his eyes
to heaven, but beat his breast, saying, 'God, be merciful to
me a sinner!' I tell you, this man went down to his house
justified rather than the other; for every one who exalts
himself will be humbled, but he who humbles himself will
be exalted."

–Luke 18:11-14

"Ask, and it will be given you; seek, and you will find; knock, and it will be opened to you. For every one who asks receives, and he who seeks finds, and to him who knocks it will be opened. Or what man of you, if his son asks him for bread, will give him a stone? Or if he asks for a fish, will give him a serpent? If you then, who are evil, know how to give good gifts to your children, how much more will your Father who is in heaven give good things to those who ask him!"

–Matthew 7:7-11

Have no anxiety about anything, but in everything by prayer and supplication with thanksgiving let your requests be made known to God. And the peace of God, which passes all understanding, will keep your hearts and your minds in Christ Jesus. Finally, brethren, whatever is true, whatever is honorable, whatever is just, whatever is pure, whatever is lovely, whatever is gracious, if there is any excellence, if there is anything worthy of praise, think about these things.

–Philippians 4:6-8

"If you abide in me, and my words abide in you, ask whatever you will, and it shall be done for you. By this my Father is glorified, that you bear much fruit, and so prove to be my disciples. As the Father has loved me, so have I loved you; abide in my love. If you keep my commandments, you will abide in my love, just as I have kept my Father's commandments and abide in his love. These things I have spoken to you, that my joy may be in you, and that your joy may be full."

–John 15:7-11

CHAPTER EIGHT

With the Help of Thy Grace: Everyday Confession

The scribes and the Pharisees brought a woman who had been caught in adultery, and placing her in their midst they said to him, "Teacher, this woman has been caught in the act of adultery. Now in the law Moses commanded us to stone such. What do you say about her?" This they said to test him, that they might have some charge to bring against him. Jesus bent down and wrote with his finger on the ground. And as they continued to ask him, he stood up and said to them, "Let him who is without sin among you be the first to throw a stone at her." And once more he bent down and wrote with his finger on the ground. But when they heard it, they went away, one by one, beginning with the eldest, and Jesus was left alone with the woman standing before him. Jesus looked up and said to her, "Woman, where are they? Has no one condemned you?"

–John 8:3-10

He said to them, "But who do you say that I am?" Simon Peter replied, "You are the Christ, the Son of the living God." And Jesus answered him, "Blessed are you, Simon Bar-Jona! For flesh and blood has not revealed this to you, but my Father who is in heaven. And I tell you, you are Peter, and on this rock I will build my Church, and the gates of Hades shall not prevail against it. I will give you the keys of the kingdom of heaven, and whatever you bind on earth shall be bound in heaven, and whatever you loose on earth shall be loosed in heaven."

–Matthew 16:15-19

He does not deal with us according to our sins,
  nor repay us according to our iniquities.
For as the heavens are high above the earth,
  so great is his mercy toward those who fear him;
as far as the east is from the west,
  so far does he remove our transgressions from us.
As a father pities his children,
  so the Lord *pities those who fear him.*
For he knows our frame;
  he remembers that we are dust.

–Psalm 103:10-14

CHAPTER NINE

God Within Us: Everyday Eucharist

So Jesus said to them, "Truly, truly, I say to you, unless you eat the flesh of the Son of man and drink his blood, you have no life in you; he who eats my flesh and drinks my blood has eternal life, and I will raise him up at the last day. For my flesh is food indeed, and my blood is drink indeed. He who eats my flesh and drinks my blood abides in me, and I in him. As the living Father sent me, and I live because of the Father, so he who eats me will live because of me. This is the bread which came down from heaven, not such as the fathers ate and died; he who eats this bread will live for ever."

–John 6:53-58

One of his disciples, Andrew, Simon Peter's brother, said to him, "There is a lad here who has five barley loaves and two fish; but what are they among so many?" Jesus said, "Make the people sit down." Now there was much grass in the place; so the men sat down, in number about five thousand. Jesus then took the loaves, and when he had given thanks, he distributed them to those who were seated; so also the fish, as much as they wanted.

–John 6:8-11

When they got out on land, they saw a charcoal fire there, with fish lying on it, and bread. Jesus said to them, "Bring some of the fish that you have just caught." Simon Peter went aboard and hauled the net ashore, full of large fish, a hundred and fifty-three of them; and although there were so many, the net was not torn. Jesus said to them, "Come and have breakfast."

–John 21:9-12

Now as they were eating, Jesus took bread, and blessed, and broke it, and gave it to the disciples and said, "Take, eat; this is my body." And he took a chalice, and when he had given thanks he gave it to them, saying, "Drink of it, all of you; for this is my blood of the covenant, which is poured out for many for the forgiveness of sins."

–Matthew 26:26-28

The cup of blessing which we bless, is it not a participation in the blood of Christ? The bread which we break, is it not a participation in the body of Christ? Because there is one bread, we who are many are one body, for we all partake of the one bread.

–1 Corinthians 10:16-17

NOTES

1 Fulton Sheen, "How to Make the Holy Hour," in *The Priest Is Not His Own* (1963; repr., San Francisco: Ignatius, 2004), books.google.com.

2 Julian of Norwich, *Revelations of Divine Love*, ed. Grace Warrack (London: Methuen, 1901), 10, gutenberg.org.

3 Quoted in Dennis Gallagher, "Ask Father: Describe the Difference Between Meditation and Contemplation," *Catholic Digest*, August 4, 2020, catholicdigest.com.

4 Maria Faustina Kowalska and the Marians of the Immaculate Conception, *Diary of Saint Maria Faustina Kowalska* (Stockbridge, MA: Marian Press, 2008), 148.

5 Faustina, 291.

6 Jacques Philippe, *In the School of the Holy Spirit*, trans. Helena Scott (New York: Scepter, 2007), 29.

7 *Story of a Soul: The Autobiography of Saint Thérèse of Lisieux*, 3rd ed., trans. John Clarke (Washington, DC: ICS, 1996), 179, emphasis removed.

8 Philippe, 45.

9 *The Way of a Pilgrim*, trans. Nina A. Toumanova (Mineola, NY: Dover, 2008), 13–14.

10 Brené Brown, "Listening to Shame," TED talk, TED2012, March 2012, 13:23, ted.com.

11 Thérèse to Marie Guerin, Letter 92, May 30, 1889, in *Letters of St. Therese of Lisieux: General Correspondence*, trans. John Clarke, vol. 1, *1877–1890* (Washington, DC: ICS, 1982), 568, books.google.com.

12 From a letter to his brother, quoted in *Kolbe: Saint of the Immaculata*, ed. Francis M. Kalvelage (San Francisco: Ignatius, 2002), 31, books. google.com.

13 *Compendium of the Catechism of the Catholic Church* (Vatican City:
    Libreria Editrice Vaticana, 2005), vatican.va.

14 *Compendium.*

15 *Compendium.*

16 *Compendium.* "First attributed to Sts. Ambrose, Augustine, or Hilary,
    it is now accredited to Nicetas, Bishop of Remesiana (4th century). It
    is used at the conclusion of the Office of the Readings for the Liturgy
    of the Hours on Sundays outside Lent, daily during the Octaves of
    Christmas and Easter, and on Solemnities and Feast Days" (Michael
    Martin, "The Te Deum," ewtn.com).

17 "Suscipe," loyolapress.com, capitalization altered.

18 John Bartunek, *The Better Part: Gospel of Luke* (Manchester, NH:
    Sophia Institute Press, 2020), 49.

19 "A Prayer of St. Ignatius Loyola," in *Catholic Prayers: Compiled from
    Traditional Sources*, ed. Thomas A. Nelson (Charlotte, NC: TAN, 2006),
    books.google.com.

20 "Prayer of St. Augustine," catholicnewsagency.com.

21 Ignatius of Loyola, "Prayer of St. Ignatius, 'Anima Christi,'" in *The
    Spiritual Exercises of Saint Ignatius, or Manresa* (TAN Classics, 2010).

22 John Henry Newman, "Meditations on Christian Doctrine: I. Hope
    in God—Creator," in *Meditations and Devotions of the Late Cardinal
    Newman* (London: Longmans, Green, 1907), newmanreader.org.

23 Quoted in Philip Kosloski, "Mother Teresa Prayed This Inspirational
    Prayer on a Daily Basis," *Aleteia* (blog), September 5, 2018, aleteia.org.

24 "Peace Prayer of Saint Francis," loyolapress.com.

25 Quoted in Michelle Jones, "Contemplating 'St. Teresa's Bookmark'
    with *The Jewish Bride*," Carmelite Institute of North America,
    carmeliteinstitute.net.

26 Quoted in Francis, *Gaudete et Exsultate* (March 19, 2018), 101n,
    vatican.va.

27 "Thomas à Kempis," in *Catholic Prayers for All Occasions*, ed. Jacquelyn
    Lindsey (Huntington, IN: Our Sunday Visitor, 2017), books.google.com.

28 *The Raccolta: Prayers and Devotions Enriched with Indulgences* (1957; repr., Fitzwilliam, NH: Loreto, 2004), 23, language modernized.

29 From "Prayer of St. Thomas Aquinas for Virtue," in *Blessed Be God: A Complete Catholic Prayer Book* (New York: P. J. Kenedy & Sons, 1925), 491, language modernized.

30 Quoted in Philip Kosloski, "This Prayer of St. Patrick Protects You in Spiritual Combat," *Aleteia* (blog), March 14, 2018, aleteia.org.

31 "St. Benedict of Nursia: For Seekers of Faith," in Lindsey.

32 "St. Anselm of Canterbury: Searching for God," in Lindsey.

33 "Prayer for the Sick," Villanova University Mission and Ministry, villanova.edu.

34 Attributed to Rafael Merry del Val (1865–1930), cardinal and secretary of state under Pope St. Pius X. The prayer is shortened here.

35 Written by Sr. Faustina Maria Pia, SV, Sisters of Life (sistersoflife. org). Please visit the website of the Sisters of Life to obtain individual copies of the litany.

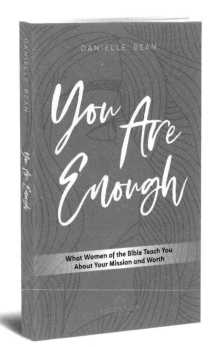